GENERATIVE AI FOR BEGINNERS PLAYBOOK

Discover Practical, Simplified, Step-By-Step Applications to Generate Just About Anything You Can Imagine

Branson Adams

Walking Crow

718 – 333 Brooksbank Ave #307

North Vancouver, BC V7J 3V8

Cataloguing data available from Library and Archives Canada

eBook ISBN: 978-1-988099-17-0

Paperback ISBN: 978-1-988099-18-7

Audio ISBN: 978-1-988099-19-4

Hard Cover ISBN: 978-1-988099-20-0

Amazon Paperback ASIN: 1988099188

Amazon Kindle ASIN: B0CWDQSC74

Amazon Hardcover ASIN: 198809920X

TABLE OF CONTENTS

INTRODUCTION:

In an era where technology is not just an aid but a vital part of our daily lives, the rise of Generative AI is a pivotal evolution in how we interact with the digital world. This transformation isn't limited to tech giants and digital savants—it's something that can and will permeate every aspect of creativity, business acumen, and personal growth. Did you know businesses adopting AI solutions have seen a 50% reduction in time spent on mundane tasks and a significant boost in creative output? These are not just numbers; they represent a growing trend that could redefine everyone's professional and personal landscapes, offering you the potential to revolutionize your own work and personal life.

As someone deeply passionate about making AI more accessible to everyone, I've crafted this playbook to demystify the seeming complexities of Generative AI and make it a practical tool for all, including you. Whether you are a seasoned businessperson, an intrigued beginner, or somewhere in between, this book is your gateway to understanding and leveraging AI to not just optimize but also revolutionize your approach to creation and problem-solving. This playbook is not just a theoretical guide; it's a practical resource designed to meet you where you are in your AI journey. It will provide you with assistance that you can apply to your work and personal life starting today.

This book will give you a solid understanding of Generative AI across various domains, including practical examples, hands-on starting points, and prompts you can use right away. From generating art and music to devising robust business strategies and enhancing personal life efficiency, this playbook covers it all. The information is presented clearly and jargon-free, so you can immediately start applying these skills in your daily life and work.

Embracing the power of AI has its ethical challenges. This book does not shy away from these critical discussions; it provides details and an approach that allows you to use AI responsibly and ethically, ensuring you are aware of the potential impact of your actions and can make informed decisions.

I encourage you to read this book and actively interact by opening a couple of accounts when directed to do so and by using the "prompts" provided. As we explore the multifaceted applications of Generative AI, from creating stunning visual art with DALL·E to drafting comprehensive business plans and engaging customer chatbots, the potential for what you can achieve with these tools is enormous.

Have fun with the tools and ideas discussed, and don't hesitate to push the boundaries of what you can create and achieve with AI. Real understanding comes from hands-on experience, and this playbook is designed to accompany that active exploration.

So jump into the realm of Generative AI with an open mind and a readiness to tap into a world of endless creative and innovative possibilities.

This book is not just about learning what AI can do—it's about discovering what you can do with AI.

CHAPTER 1:
DEMYSTIFYING GENERATIVE AI

Did you know that the stunning visuals in your favorite sci-fi movie or the catchy tune from a viral ad might not have been entirely created by humans? Welcome to the intriguing world of Generative AI, where the line between human and machine creativity blurs, offering endless possibilities. This isn't just about robots taking over jobs; it's about leveraging technology to push the boundaries of what we can create and achieve. This chapter will strip away the complexities of Generative AI, making it accessible, understandable, and ready for you to use in ways you might not have imagined yet.

1.1 WHAT IS GENERATIVE AI? SIMPLIFYING THE COMPLEX

Definition and Scope:

Generative AI is a subset of artificial intelligence technologies that can generate new content—from images and music to text and beyond. It's like having an incredibly versatile artist at your disposal, one who doesn't get tired and continually learns from the best. But it's not magic—it's science. These systems use algorithms that learn from vast amounts of existing data to produce new, original outputs that can sometimes pass for human-made.

Core Principles:

At the core of Generative AI is the principle of learning from vast amounts of data. Imagine a system that scans through thousands of paintings or listens to countless music tracks. Over time, it picks up on patterns, styles, and nuances that define different genres or artists. It then uses this accumulated data to create something new that feels familiar yet fresh. This ability to learn and generate makes Generative AI an invaluable tool in creative processes, offering a blend of precision and innovation that was previously hard to achieve.

Types of Generative AI:

Let's talk about the types of Generative AI that are making waves. First up, Generative Adversarial Networks, or GANs. Picture two AI systems set against each other—one generates content while the other evaluates it. This back-and-forth ensures the end product is incredibly refined. Then, there are Variational Autoencoders (VAEs), which are great at generating complex data like photographs by learning how to encode data into smaller, compressed representations and then decoding it back to the original form. These are not the only models, but they are the models we will focus on most closely, and each has unique strengths that make them suitable for different creative tasks.

Real-world Implications:

The impact of Generative AI stretches far beyond just creating art. It's revolutionizing industries by enabling new forms of content creation that are faster, more cost-effective, and often just as good as (or even better than) what humans can create on their own. In fashion, designers use AI to develop groundbreaking styles and patterns. In advertising, companies use AI to generate content that resonates better with different audiences. Even in education, Generative AI helps create interactive and personalized learning materials that can adapt to the learning pace of students. These applications are not about replacing human creativity but enhancing it, opening new opportunities for innovation and efficiency.

Interactive Element: Experiment with Generative AI: Why not try it yourself to get a real feeling for what Generative AI can do? Here's a simple exercise to make a precursory exploration into Generative AI: Visit an AI art generator online, such as Openai's DALL·E and open an account (https://openart.ai/ - many are freely accessible), and input a description of a scene you'd like to visualize. You'll see how the AI interprets and brings your words to life in an image. Then, you can play around with different descriptions and compare the image outputs. This hands-on experience will give you a glimpse into the creative potential of AI. It might spark some ideas about how to use it in your projects or business.

In case you'd like some help, here are a couple of starter examples you can try:

- **Prompt for a Peaceful Landscape**: "Generate an image of a serene landscape during sunset. The scene includes a calm lake reflecting the vibrant colors of the sky, surrounded by tall mountains and a few scattered pine trees. The sky should be a mix of orange, pink, and purple hues, and there should be a small wooden boat floating gently on the lake."

- **Prompt for a Whimsical Character Illustration**: "Create an image of a whimsical forest creature that resembles a mix between a fox and an owl. The creature should have the body and fur of a fox, bright orange in color, and the face and wings of an owl with striking blue feathers. It is sitting on a mossy rock, holding a small, glowing lantern with its tail, in the middle of a misty, enchanted forest at dusk."

These are simple examples of the many ways that you can input prompts into Gen AI to optimize for your desired results. A good rule of thumb is to provide at least three parameters within a Generative

AI prompt. It is important to note that receiving the exact result you want can entail honing the AI output and iterating the prompt process with various changes. It may be that you need to add or subtract parameters from your prompt. You can simply tell the Gen AI that it should keep certain elements of its output, insert additional parameters, and get a new result. This process of refinement will better enable you to receive your desired outcome. Exploring Generative AI is like opening the door to a new realm of possibilities where traditional constraints no longer limit your creative vision. Whether you're looking to innovate in your current field, explore new creative avenues, or understand the future of technology, understanding Generative AI is a crucial step. And as you'll see in the coming sections, the ways you can apply this technology are as varied and expansive as your imagination.

1.2 HISTORY AND EVOLUTION OF GENERATIVE AI (SKIP THIS SECTION IF YOU'RE NOT INTERESTED)

Let's stroll down memory lane to understand how Generative AI became the powerhouse it is today. It's like piecing together a fascinating puzzle of human ingenuity and technological evolution. The roots of Generative AI are intertwined with the early days of artificial intelligence, dating back to the mid-20th century. Picture this: it's the 1950s, and early AI researchers are beginning to theorize and experiment with machines that could one day mimic human intelligence. The Dartmouth Conference marked this era in 1956, when the term 'Artificial Intelligence' was coined, setting the stage for decades of groundbreaking work.

Fast forward a few decades to when the first practical implementations of AI began to surface. During the 1980s and 1990s, AI research had its ups and downs, often referred to as the 'AI Winter' due to reduced funding and interest. However, the seeds for future AI breakthroughs were sown during these periods of ebb and flow.

Researchers were steadily laying down the mathematical and theoretical foundations for what would later evolve into Generative AI.

As we moved into the 21st century, computational power significantly increased, and data became more accessible. This environment was ripe for AI to flourish. Whereas previously, in order to make a system perform a task, Developers had to painstakingly program systems with datasets. Yet with the development of Deep Learning (DL) in the early 2000s, systems began to learn to perform tasks directly from images, text, or sound. It was a game-changer for Generative AI. This period marked the beginning of AI's ability to analyze, generate, and create, leading to the development of sophisticated models like GANs (Generative Adversarial Networks) introduced by Ian Goodfellow and his colleagues in 2014. These networks, which involve two neural networks contesting with each other to generate new, synthetic instances of data, revolutionized the field by producing startlingly realistic results. An example of one result is the emergence of Deepfakes, images or videos of "real people," saying things they did not actually say. Obviously, this breeches ethical boundaries, which I'll talk more about later.

In recent years, the advancements in Generative AI have accelerated at a breathtaking pace. Just look at tools like GPT-4 for text generation or DALL-E for image creation. These tools have captured the public's imagination and shown the creative potential of AI. They are not just academic experiments but are being integrated into various industries, reshaping how content is created, personalized, and consumed. The ability of AI to learn from existing data and generate new content that is indistinguishable from human-generated content has massive implications for creative industries, among many others.

The future of Generative AI holds limitless possibilities. As computational methods grow more powerful and datasets become more nuanced, the next generation of Generative AI will be more refined and capable of further amplification and enhancement of human creativity. We might see AI that can collaborate with humans to co-create art pieces that blend human emotion and AI precision, or AI systems that can innovate new scientific theories or compose complex pieces of music with emotional depth. The potential for these technologies to expand human creativity and problem-solving is immense, and we are just scratching the surface.

AI Opens Many Doors

What's particularly exciting as we look to the future is how these advancements will make Generative AI even more accessible to non-experts. Simplified interfaces and more intuitive controls mean that anyone with a creative vision could soon harness AI's power to bring their ideas to life, regardless of their education or technical ability. This democratization of technology promises to level the playing field, allowing for a diversity of voices and perspectives to be heard and realized in ways we might not have imagined just a few decades ago.

As we continue to push the boundaries of what's possible with Generative AI, it's important to stay grounded in ethical considerations. The power of AI to generate and create is a double-edged sword. As we innovate, we must safeguard against misuse and ensure that advancements contribute positively to society. Whether it's ensuring the unbiased training of AI models or the ethical use of AI-generated content, the responsibility lies with all of us to steer the future of Generative AI in a direction that enhances and enriches human capabilities without overshadowing them.

1.3 Understanding AI, Machine Learning, and Deep Learning

Diving into the world of AI can sometimes feel like you're learning a new language. Let's break it down into simpler terms, focusing on how these technologies pave the way for something as innovative as Generative AI. Artificial Intelligence, or AI, is a significant umbrella term that covers any technology that enables machines to mimic human behavior. Under this broad category, we have subsets like Machine Learning (ML) and Deep Learning (DL), which play a massive role in developing AI applications, including those that generate new content like text, images, and music.

Since your smartphone is the most frequent technology you interact with, let's think of AI as your smartphone. Now, machine learning (ML) is like the apps on your phone that learn from your behavior to improve their functions—for example, a shopping app that suggests products based on your past purchases. ML algorithms use statistical methods to enable machines to improve tasks with experience. Essentially, they learn from past computations to produce reliable, repeatable decisions and results—it's a form of AI that allows a system to learn from data rather than through explicit programming. However, it doesn't just learn; it adapts. Every new piece of data has the potential to alter its understanding and functioning.

Deep Learning (DL), a subset of machine learning, takes this a step further. It uses structures called neural networks that are inspired by the human brain. Just as we use our brains to recognize patterns and classify different types of information, neural networks identify patterns in data. They interpret sensory data through machine perception, labeling, or clustering raw input. These algorithms can recognize faces, translate languages, and even generate human-like text based on what they have learned from vast datasets.

Now, let's talk about how these systems learn from data because that's where it gets exciting. Machine learning models get better over time by absorbing and analyzing new data. For instance, an ML model designed to predict stock prices is fed vast amounts of historical stock market data; it analyzes this data to identify patterns or trends that were successful in the past and uses this information to make predictions about future stock prices. Deep learning models work similarly but can digest and analyze more complex data thanks to their deep neural networks. They can handle unstructured data like images, sound, and text more effectively, making them ideal for tasks like voice recognition in virtual assistance or content recommendation in streaming services.

Understanding the distinctions between machine learning and deep learning is crucial, especially in the context of generative AI. While both are under the AI umbrella, deep learning is more sophisticated and capable of learning from large amounts of unstructured data. This makes it particularly good at tasks that require understanding complex, human-like nuances, such as generating realistic speech in different languages or creating high-resolution, lifelike images from textual descriptions alone.

These technologies have practical applications that touch almost every aspect of modern life. In healthcare, machine learning models predict patient diagnoses based on symptoms and medical history, significantly improving the speed and accuracy of patient care. In the entertainment industry, deep learning powers the algorithms that recommend what movies or TV shows you might enjoy next on streaming platforms. In the automotive sector, deep learning drives the development of autonomous vehicles, teaching cars to recognize and react to their surroundings to navigate safely. Elon Musk recently spoke on Tesla's Dojo (FSD V12), their self-driving AI, stating that it has also been trained to and does read—in every language in the world—to maintain the ability to recognize and react appropriately to navigate safely. Fascinating Developments.

Through these examples, it's clear that AI, machine learning, and deep learning aren't just futuristic concepts but are actively shaping our world today. They are making tasks more manageable, processes faster, and outcomes better across various industries. Whether optimizing logistics, enhancing personalized shopping experiences, or advancing scientific research, these technologies provide the backbone for much of our digital transformation. They allow businesses to operate more efficiently and offer more personalized user experiences, making understanding these technologies precious for tech professionals and anyone looking to enhance their career or business in the digital age.

1.4 KEY TECHNOLOGIES BEHIND GENERATIVE AI

This may be a bit technical, but stick with me—it will be illuminating, especially if you're keen to understand how Generative AI does its magic. At the heart of this technology are neural networks, a series of algorithms that attempt to recognize underlying relationships in a data set through a process that mimics how the human brain operates. Imagine you're trying to teach a toddler to identify different fruits. You show them several examples of apples and oranges, and gradually, they learn to categorize and recognize the fruits. Similarly, neural networks process huge amounts of data, understand patterns and features, and use this knowledge to make decisions or generate new data that mimics the original data's style and properties.

Neural networks are crucial for creating generative AI models because they handle and interpret the complexity of the data involved. Whether it's the subtleties of human language or the intricate patterns of a digital image, neural networks analyze the data and generate new instances that are remarkably accurate and often indistinguishable from what a human might produce. They consist of layers of nodes, each designed to recognize different aspects of the data. The first layer might recognize simple features, while deeper layers interpret more complex elements. This hierarchical structure allows the network to handle everything from simplest to highly complex generation tasks.

As we touched on earlier, , Generative Adversarial Networks (GANs) and Variational Autoencoders (VAEs) are neural networks specifically pivotal in Generative AI. GANs' functions are particularly fascinating; they consist of two neural networks contesting with one another. One network, the generator, creates data, while the other, the discriminator, evaluates it. The generator learns to produce more convincing data over time through their rivalry. This method has created everything from photorealistic images to innovative fashion designs. VAEs, on the other hand, are great at learning complex data distributions. They work by compressing data into a smaller, more straightforward form and then expanding it back to its original form, effectively learning the essential traits of the data.

The surge in computational power over recent years has significantly propelled the capabilities of these networks. Today's computers can process and analyze data at unprecedented speeds and scales, allowing for training large, complex neural networks in reasonable times. This increased computational power means that tasks that would have taken years to compute on older machines can now be done in days or even hours. It's like having the ability to run thousands of experiments simultaneously, drastically speeding up the innovation and refinement process in AI development.

Then there's the role of data—arguably as crucial as the AI models themselves. Generative AI requires vast amounts of data to learn effectively. This data is the raw material from which the AI learns to generate new content. However, the availability and quality of this data are critical. The more comprehensive and diverse the dataset, the better the AI can learn and the more nuanced the output. The challenge lies in gathering high-quality, unbiased data that can be used to train these systems effectively. In many cases, the data must be curated and processed to ensure that it is helpful for training purposes, which can be labor-intensive.

CHAPTER 2:
GENERATIVE AI IN PRACTICE

Have you ever wondered how some online articles seem to write themselves? Or how personalized ads always seem to know what you're interested in? Welcome to the world of Generative AI in text creation. It's like having a super-smart assistant who writes and tailors content specifically for you, revolutionizing how we create and consume text. From automating mundane writing tasks to crafting engaging marketing copy, Generative AI is here to transform your work. In the upcoming chapters, I'll guide you through various AI platforms, but in this chapter, I'll lay the groundwork for your exploration.

2.1 TRANSFORMING TEXT: FROM WRITING TO CONTENT CREATION

Content Generation:

Imagine you're running a bustling online business but need help keeping up with the demand for content. Enter Generative AI. This technology is a game-changer for creating written content at scale. Whether it's drafting informative blog posts, generating engaging news articles, or even piecing together creative stories, AI tools are stepping up. They work by learning from vast databases of existing text and then applying this knowledge to generate new content that matches a given prompt or style. For example, suppose you feed a generative AI system a prompt about the latest fashion trends. In that case, it can produce an entire article with style tips and industry insights in seconds. This speeds up content creation and helps maintain a steady stream of fresh content to keep your audience engaged.

Language Models:

At the heart of this text transformation are advanced algorithms known as language models, with GPT-3/4 being one of the most popular. Developed by OpenAI, GPT-4 can understand and generate human-like text-based input. It's like chatting with someone who knows a little about everything under the sun. The power of GPT-4 lies in its ability to process and generate text in a way that feels incredibly natural and relevant. This capability makes it an invaluable tool for applications ranging from writing assistance to customer service bots, where understanding context and delivering appropriate responses is vital. Sam Altman, the Open AI CEO, referred to ChatGPT as a reasoning engine, in the same way that Google search is a search engine.

Personalization:

One of the most captivating aspects of AI in text creation is its ability to personalize content. Have you ever noticed how some websites seem to speak directly to you? That's AI at work. By analyzing data on your past interactions, preferences, and even the nuances in your choice of words, AI can tailor content to suit your unique tastes or needs. This personalized approach enhances user engagement and amplifies the effectiveness of marketing campaigns by delivering messages that resonate on a more personal level with the audience, making them feel understood and catered to.

Challenges and Solutions:

Integrating AI into your content strategy can be challenging. One primary concern is ensuring the accuracy of the information generated. AI models can produce content that is factually incorrect or contextually inappropriate. Another issue is the potential for generating misleading or biased content, especially if the AI has been trained on skewed data sets. Human oversight is crucial to address these concerns. By setting up robust review processes and continually training your AI on a diverse range of high-quality, accurate data, you can minimize errors and ensure the content remains trustworthy and unbiased. Additionally, tools are being developed to automatically fact-check and neutralize bias in AI-generated content, helping maintain high standards of accuracy and fairness.

Interactive Element: Generate Your AI Content

Are you curious to see Generative AI in action? Here's a simple exercise. Visit ChatGPT at https://chat.openai.com/; Openai's text generator. Create an account and ask a question about a topic you're interested in. It could be anything from "tips for first-time pet owners" to "how to start a podcast." Writing a sentence of instructions for your AI platform is known as a "prompt," and we'll talk more about prompts later. Watch as the AI crafts a piece of content right before your eyes. Then ask it to say the same thing but give a "tone" you'd like it to write in, such as authoritative, friendly, or funny, and see how the AI adapts. This hands-on experience will give you a glimpse into the capabilities of AI-driven content creation and spark ideas on how to integrate this technology into your content strategy.

As we continue to explore the capabilities and applications of Generative AI in text creation, it's clear that this technology is set to play a pivotal role in shaping the future of written content. Whether it's enhancing creativity, personalizing user experiences, or streamlining content production, the possibilities are as expansive as they are exciting. And while challenges remain, the ongoing advancements in AI technology promise to open up even more opportunities for innovation in content creation. So, whether you're a content creator looking to optimize your workflow, a business looking to better engage with your customers, or just someone curious about the future of AI in writing, the journey into the world of AI-driven text generation will be rewarding.

2.2 REVOLUTIONIZING ART: HOW AI IS CREATING NEW FORMS OF ART

Imagine stepping into a gallery where the art on the walls isn't just the product of brushes and palettes but the intricate algorithms of generative AI. This isn't a scene from a futuristic movie; it's a reality that's unfolding right now. Artists worldwide are embracing AI, not merely as a tool, but as a creative partner, pushing the boundaries of their craft to produce works that span from surreal digital landscapes to hyper-realistic portraits. Generative AI in visual arts isn't just about automating creativity; it's about expanding the human artistic experience, empowering creators to delve into complex patterns and aesthetics that were once unimaginable or excessively time-consuming to achieve manually.

Artists use generative AI to create visual art by feeding algorithms with vast amounts of visual data, teaching them to recognize and replicate complex artistic styles. These AI systems can generate original pieces that reflect learned styles or combine them to create something new. Imagine an AI that has studied every known Picasso and Van Gogh painting; it can then blend these styles to create a striking new piece that evokes familiar artistic sensibilities. Moreover, AI is used to create digital sculptures and installations that interact with environments and audiences dynamically, transforming how we experience art.

The collaboration between AI and artists is a fascinating dance of give-and-take. In some projects, artists set broad parameters and let the AI run wild, later curating its outputs to select pieces that resonate with their vision. In others, the AI's role is more nuanced, suggesting alterations and variations to a human artist's initial designs, thereby acting as a co-creator. These collaborations are proving to be a goldmine for creativity, often resulting in artworks that challenge our perceptions of art and creativity. For instance, the 'Next Rembrandt' project involved teaching a system to paint like Rembrandt. Using data from his existing works, the AI didn't just mimic Rembrandt's style; it created an entirely new piece that could easily pass as one of the master's lost works. This project showcased AI's creative potential and sparked a conversation about creativity and machine involvement.

However, with the rise of AI in art, a heated debate around the originality and authorship of AI-generated art has also surfaced. Who is the real artist when an AI creates a piece of art? This is rampant across all artistic endeavors. Authors, artists, musicians, videographers, and more have expressed outrage and dismay at AI systems "copying," "pirating," and even simply being trained on their proprietary works. This is a complex and nuanced discussion. Is it the algorithm's creator, the AI, or the artist who conceptualized the project? These questions challenge our traditional understanding of art as a purely human endeavor. Moreover, copyright and intellectual property issues arise when AI creates art that could be indistinguishably similar to works created by humans. The art community and legal experts are wrestling with these questions, trying to establish norms and guidelines that recognize both human and machine contributions to creative works.

Navigating this new terrain, artists and technologists are continually developing tools and platforms that harness the capabilities of generative AI. These range from simple web-based applications that allow users to generate AI art with a few clicks to more sophisticated systems that can be integrated into professional workflows. Tools such as RunwayML provide creatives with an intuitive interface to experiment with generative models, allowing them to integrate AI into their art without needing a background in coding. Similarly, platforms like Artbreeder enable users to merge various images to create complex digital artworks that the community can continually evolve. These tools are not just expanding the accessibility of AI technology in the arts; they are also fostering a new culture of collaborative and participatory creation.

As we continue to explore and push the limits of what artificial intelligence can achieve in art, the narrative of AI as merely a tool is rapidly evolving. AI is becoming a collaborator, an instigator of new forms of expression, and a provocateur challenging our definitions of creativity and authorship. The implications of this shift are profound, touching on philosophical, ethical, and practical realms, ensuring that the discourse around AI in art remains as dynamic and evolving as the technology itself. Whether viewed as a threat to traditional artistic methods or a catalyst for unprecedented creative exploration, generative AI undeniably reshapes the artistic landscape, inviting artists and audiences to reconsider their roles in the interactive tapestry of creation and interpretation.

2.3 THE SOUND OF INNOVATION: GENERATIVE AI IN MUSIC PRODUCTION

Imagine a world where your favorite playlist is not just tailored to your tastes but created for you, note by note, by an intelligent system that understands your moods and preferences. This is not a distant future scenario; it's happening now, thanks to generative AI in music production. This technology is being used to compose original music, generate unique sounds, and even perform in ways that were once strictly human domains.

Generative AI steps into the music studio with algorithms that can learn styles from a vast array of existing music then generate new compositions that are at the intersection of fresh and familiar. These

AI systems use deep learning to analyze everything from melody and harmony to rhythm and tempo, capturing the essence of music genres in incredible detail. They can then create new music that resonates with these learned patterns with a new twist. For instance, AI has been instrumental in creating music for video games where it can produce tracks that adapt to the gameplay, enhancing the player's experience without needing constant human input. In live performances, AI-generated music is beginning to take center stage, with algorithms responding in real-time to the audience's reactions or other performers' music, creating an interactive experience that was hardly imaginable a few years ago.

Collaborations between musicians and AI are pushing these boundaries even further, transforming not just how music is made but also how it's perceived. Artists are increasingly partnering with AI to explore new creative possibilities. These collaborations often see the artist prompt the AI with initial themes, motifs, or even emotional cues. The AI then processes the input to produce music that might take the artist in new and unexpected directions. This partnership can be potent in live settings, where AI can instantly generate music in response to the changing dynamics of the performance, providing a level of improvisation traditionally associated with seasoned musicians. One notable example is the collaboration between the composer Benoit Carré and AI software, which resulted in the first AI Eurovision song, demonstrating that AI can participate creatively in highly complex musical compositions.

Personalized customization of music is another area AI significantly impacts. Streaming services use AI to analyze your listening habits and suggest new songs and artists you might like, but generative AI takes this a step further. It can create music that adapts to real-time feedback, skipping beats, or slowing down the tempo as per your current activity or even your heart rate, which fitness apps might use to enhance your workout experience. Imagine a morning run where the music's pace matches your steps or a meditation session where the background tracks sync with your breathing patterns. AI is making this level of personalized musical experience possible.

However, the involvement of AI in music production has its challenges, particularly in the realm of copyright ethics. As AI becomes more capable of creating music that closely resembles the style or even specific works of human artists, questions arise about AI-created works' originality and the associated rights. Copyright laws traditionally protect human creators, but as AI plays a more significant role in the creative process, redefining what it means to be a creator becomes imperative. Is the programmer who designed the AI entitled to rights, or should copyright belong to the user who provided the initial input? Or should the AI itself be seen as the creator? These are ethical questions and practical concerns that must be addressed as AI-generated music becomes more common and commercially viable.

Navigating these issues involves a careful balance between encouraging innovation and protecting the rights of human artists. Legal frameworks worldwide are beginning to catch up, with ongoing discussions about the best ways to integrate AI into the creative industries without stifling human creativity. As we move forward, these discussions will be crucial in shaping a music industry that can embrace the benefits of AI while ensuring fair practices for all creators, human and artificial alike. As AI continues to evolve, its role in music production promises to be as dynamic and impactful as the music it helps create, offering new opportunities for artists to explore and audiences to enjoy.

2.4 BRINGING IMAGINATIONS TO LIFE WITH AI-GENERATED ANIMATION

Imagine your favorite cartoon or the most breathtaking animated movie you've ever seen. Now, consider the possibility that AI could be the driving force behind bringing such vibrant characters and dynamic scenes to life. Traditionally, animation had been a labor-intensive process involving countless hours of designing, rendering, and tweaking to bring a single character to life. However, with the advent of AI in this creative industry, the paradigm is shifting dramatically.

In the realm of animation, generative AI is making significant strides, transforming how animations are created, from the initial concept to the final colorful frames that hit the screen. animation

AI, particularly in animation, is a powerful tool that automates many time-consuming tasks that bog down the animation process. Using machine learning algorithms, generative AI can animate complex scenes and characters with a level of fluidity and realism that can be hard to achieve manually. For instance, AI algorithms can take a basic sketch of a character, refine its design, and animate it across various scenes, maintaining consistent lighting, shadows, and movements that resonate with the character's emotions and the story's ambiance. This capability significantly reduces the time and cost associated with traditional animation techniques, allowing studios to produce high-quality animations faster and more economically.

This surge in efficiency does not come at the expense of creativity—quite the opposite. AI in animation catalyzes a new frontier of creative freedom for animators and designers. With AI handling the more mundane aspects of animation, creatives can focus more on their projects' artistry and storytelling components. They can easily experiment with different styles, narratives, and character designs, knowing that AI can quickly help prototype and bring these ideas to life. This freedom to experiment without the typical constraints of time and resources means that animators can push the boundaries of conventional animation to create unique, innovative content that stands out in a crowded media landscape.

Integrating AI technologies into the animation workflow is becoming more prevalent across various sectors, not just in film but also in video games and virtual reality. In video games, AI-driven animation allows for more dynamic and responsive environments. Characters can move and react in real-time to player actions in an incredibly lifelike and immersive way. In virtual reality, AI animations can adapt to the viewer's interactions, providing a profoundly personalized experience that enhances the sense of presence and engagement. Major studios and independent creators harness these AI capabilities to develop more interactive and captivating animation experiences, setting new standards for producing and consuming animated content.

Looking toward the future, the possibilities of AI-generated animation are as vast as they are exciting. We are likely to see AI enhancing the efficiency of animation production and playing a crucial role in shaping narrative techniques and visual aesthetics. AI could lead to the development of new genres of animated content that blend human creativity with machine intelligence in ways we have yet to fully imagine. Furthermore, as AI technology evolves, its integration into animation could lead to more personalized and adaptive content. Imagine animated films that change in real-time according to audience reactions or educational animations that adapt to student's learning pace and preferences. These advancements could redefine the role of animation in entertainment and education, making it more interactive, engaging, and tailored to individual viewers.

As we continue to explore and innovate within this space, the impact of AI on animation promises to be profound, offering both challenges and opportunities. It invites animators, technologists, and storytellers to rethink the traditional animation processes and explore new creative landscapes freed by AI. This evolving synergy between human creativity and artificial intelligence is not just transforming animation but is also setting the stage for a new era of digital storytelling.

2.5 Voice Generation: Speaking with the Tongue of AI

The realm of voice technology has taken a transformative leap forward with the advent of generative AI, crafting voices that are not just synthetic but strikingly lifelike. Picture this: a voice that can laugh, express sorrow, or show excitement, all generated by AI. This leap in technology is not just about creating any voice, but voices that resonate with human emotions and subtleties, making digital interactions increasingly seamless and natural.

Generative AI can produce synthetic voices that are customizable, that capture the nuances that make each voice unique. This involves sophisticated algorithms that learn from human voice data, capturing everything from pitch and tone to emotional inflections. The result is a synthetic voice that can perform various roles, whether reading out your daily news in a soothing tone or guiding you through a meditation session with gentle reassurance. The technology behind this is fascinating and incredibly potent in its applications, reshaping how we interact with machines.

One of the most prominent applications of AI-generated voices is in audiobooks. Traditionally, recording audiobooks involved hours of studio time with human narrators, but AI voices are changing the game. These voices bring stories to life with the emotional depth required to engage listeners, making the narrative journey an immersive experience. What's more, AI can provide voices for many characters, each distinct and full of personality, without hiring multiple voice actors.

Virtual assistants powered by AI are becoming increasingly sophisticated, moving beyond mere voice commands to becoming proactive helpers around the house or in the office. They can remind you of meetings, suggest the best routes to work, or even order groceries—all with a voice that often sounds pleasantly human. The technology has also been a boon for customer service, where AI bots handle inquiries and provide support with a patience that is, quite literally, programmed. This enhances customer experience, streamlines operations, and reduces the workload on human staff.

Among these advancements, the technology's ability to capture and replicate emotional nuances stands out. AI-generated voices can now convey a wide range of human emotions, making interactions more engaging. For instance, a customer service bot can detect frustration in a customer's voice and respond in an empathetic and soothing tone. Similarly, a virtual tutor can use encouraging tones to motivate students. This emotional intelligence is key to making AI interactions feel more natural and less robotic.

The power to replicate human emotion in synthetic voices comes with significant ethical considerations. One primary concern is consent, especially when it comes to replicating the voices of real people. Is using someone's voice without permission ethical, even if technology allows it? There's also the potential for misuse, such as creating misleading or harmful audio content that someone could use to deceive or defraud people. These concerns are not just hypothetical but real issues that need addressing as this technology becomes more widespread.

To navigate these ethical waters, developers and users of voice-generating AI must operate with a clear set of guidelines that respect individual rights and prioritize transparency and accountability. For instance, explicit consent should be obtained before replicating any individual's voice, and users should be notified when they interact with an AI-generated voice. Moreover, ongoing efforts to ensure that these technologies are used responsibly can help mitigate risks and foster an environment where the benefits of voice-generating AI can be enjoyed without compromising ethical standards.

As we wrap up this exploration of voice-generating AI, the advancements we've discussed are not just enhancing our interactions with technology but are reshaping them. From audiobooks and virtual assistants to customer service bots, the applications are as varied as they are impactful, offering a glimpse into a future where AI voices are an integral part of our daily lives. With its ability to understand and replicate human emotions, this technology promises a revolution in how we communicate with the digital world, making it more personal, engaging, and, ultimately, more human.

The conversation around voice-generating AI will continue evolving as this technology advances. The ethical considerations we've touched on will play a crucial role in shaping this future, ensuring that as we continue to develop these remarkable tools, we do so with a keen awareness of their broader impact on society. As we turn the page to the next chapter, we'll delve deeper into how AI is transforming our present and poised to redefine our future in ways we are only beginning to imagine.

These technologies and resources have set the stage for Generative AI to revolutionize how we create and interact with digital content. From the neural networks that provide the framework for learning and generation to the computational power that drives these processes and the data that fuels them, each component plays a pivotal role in shaping the capabilities and applications of Generative AI. As we continue to advance in these areas, the potential for what can be achieved expands, promising a future where AI's creative and generative abilities are limited only by our imagination.

CHAPTER 3:
WRITING WITH AI: FROM STORIES TO CODE

Have you ever considered writing a novel or sprucing up your blog with fresh content? What if you could turbocharge your writing creativity with a bit of AI magic? That's right, the realm of Generative AI isn't just about creating art or music; it's also revolutionizing how we write. Whether you're looking to craft the next bestseller or want to get your ideas down on paper more fluidly, AI tools are here to push your creative boundaries and unleash new possibilities in storytelling. Let's try some out.

3.1 CRAFTING STORIES WITH AI: A BEGINNER'S GUIDE

Introduction to AI Storytelling Tools

Let's start by diving into the world of AI storytelling tools. These aren't your average text processors. Imagine software that doesn't just help you correct grammar but suggests ways to deepen your plot or enrich your characters. Tools like OpenAI's GPT-4 have been designed to understand and generate human-like text based on the input they receive. This means you can feed them a story outline. They can help you flesh it out, or you can give them a character sketch. They offer back dialogue, actions, and even plot suggestions that keep your narrative moving. The beauty of these tools lies in their ability to learn from a vast expanse of literature and writing styles, making them valuable co-writers who've read more books than you could in ten lifetimes!

Setting Up Your Workspace

Before you start typing away, setting up your workspace with the right software and tools is crucial. First, choose a writing tool that integrates AI capabilities. Programs like Scrivener or Microsoft Word are great for organizing and drafting. Platforms like ShortlyAI or Sudowrite might be your best bet for AI-assisted writing as they offer more advanced AI features tailored for creative writing. A stable internet connection is also a must, as most AI writing tools operate online and require access to their AI servers to function optimally.

If you plan to use AI for creative writing, set up an account with some of these platforms and see which you like best.

Using ChatGPT

Now, let's talk about using ChatGPT for writing. ChatGPT can be a fantastic tool for brainstorming and developing ideas. Unlike other writing platforms that focus more on correcting or organizing text, ChatGPT excels in generating and expanding content. You can start by asking it to brainstorm ideas on a given theme before using one of the platforms I just mentioned. Or, if you're stuck with writer's block, ask it to suggest plot advancements based on your current storyline. Its ability to generate diverse and coherent text based on prompts makes it an excellent tool for overcoming creative hurdles and adding depth to your stories.

Research With ChatGPT

But ChatGPT isn't just for writing; it's also beneficial for research. Are you working on a historical novel? ChatGPT can quickly fetch relevant historical facts, offer character name suggestions appropriate to the era, or describe period attire.

However, just like there are practical issues with letting Copilot write your full code for you without checking its work, there are issues with ChatGPT writing factual information.

ChatGPT's output is truly remarkable, but it still sometimes provides non-factual data, that developers have termed "hallucinations."

Because of the AI's ability to extrapolate patterns at a very high level, there are times that it seems to assume that something has followed a pattern when in point of fact or in historical fact, it has not. Due to the AI's ability to provide non-factual data, or hallucinate, a person must still fact-check any data ChatGPT provides of which a person is uncertain of the validity.

For science fiction, it can provide insights into scientific concepts or future technology trends that can give your story credibility and flair. The key here is to ask specific questions; the more precise you are, the better the responses you'll get.

Developing Characters and Plots with AI

One of the most exciting uses of AI in writing is developing characters and plots. AI can help you create detailed character profiles by suggesting backstories, personality traits, and motivations that align with your story's setting and theme. It can also propose complex plot structures by weaving together multiple narrative threads, ensuring a rich and engaging storyline. This is particularly helpful if you want to add layers to your narrative but need help integrating subplots effectively.

Collaborative Storytelling

AI tools also open new avenues for collaborative storytelling. Using AI, you can explore different narrative paths or experiment with various stylistic choices, seeing in real time how changes might affect your story's progression. This can be incredibly liberating, allowing you to try multiple creative approaches quickly before deciding which direction to pursue in your writing.

Open a ChatGPT Account

Getting started with this technology is easier than you might think. If you haven't already, open a ChatGPT account and begin experimenting. Start with basic prompts to get a feel for how the AI responds. For example, you could ask it to write a short paragraph about a city in the future or describe a day in the life of a pirate. This initial interaction will help you understand the extent of ChatGPT's capabilities and how you can mold its outputs to suit your creative needs.

Four Example Prompts

To give you a head start, here are four example prompts that you can use with ChatGPT to enhance your writing projects. As you can see, you are using simple language to generate the results you are after:

1. "Generate a dialogue between two characters, one a seasoned detective and the other a nervous witness, about a mysterious disappearance." (you can be more specific about the disappearance if you like)

2. "Describe a futuristic city where technology controls nature, focusing on visual elements and atmosphere."

3. "Create a tense scene in a courtroom where a pivotal piece of evidence comes to light, shifting the trial's direction."

4. "Develop a character backstory for a rebel leader in a dystopian world, including key life events that shaped their beliefs and actions."

Each of these prompts is designed to help you explore different aspects of storytelling, from character development to world-building and plot construction. As you interact with AI, remember it's a tool meant to enhance your creativity, assist, inspire, and challenge you to push your creative boundaries. The content the AI has generated is not set in stone. It's important to modify the AI's suggestions, merge them with your ideas, or use them as springboards for entirely new concepts. See where it takes you; there's no wrong answer. AI can generate various options if you ask it to. The goal is to make writing easier, more exciting, and more fulfilling. Additionally, it's very important to modify your prompts in order to refine the AI output. This can be done by creating a whole new prompt or, by asking the platform to modify the result.

Let's say you asked ChatGPT something like this: "Write a book review of the book Generative AI for Beginners Playbook" and it gave you its response in a long paragraph form. If the response was too long, too short or not quite what you thought you'd like to say, you could refine your prompt by saying; "make that a bit shorter and in two paragraphs. When you begin to interact with AI, you'll find your output more refined and possibly closer to what you're after.

3.2 USING JASPER FOR CONTENT CREATION: A STEP-BY-STEP APPROACH

Let's switch gears and dive into another fascinating AI tool that boosts your content creation game—Jasper. Imagine you have a virtual assistant who helps you brainstorm ideas and draft content that aligns seamlessly with your style and tone. Jasper does just that, making it a go-to resource for anyone looking to enhance their content, whether for blogs, social media, or marketing materials. It's like having a creative partner ready to pitch in, ensuring you never face a blank page alone.

Overview of Jasper

Jasper, formerly known as Jarvis, is a cutting-edge content generation tool that leverages advanced AI to produce high-quality written content across various formats. What sets Jasper apart is its ability to understand context and nuance, allowing it to generate content that isn't just grammatically correct; it is engaging and tailored to your specific audience. This ensures that your content isn't just filler but drives engagement and adds value to your readers or customers.

Getting Started with Jasper

Setting up an account with Jasper is straightforward, but like any powerful tool, getting the most out of it requires setting it up correctly. First, head to their website, (jasper.ai), and sign up for an account. Jasper offers a free trial but is a paid service offering different plans based on your needs. You can choose one that fits the scale of your projects. Once your account is active, take a moment to familiarize yourself with the dashboard. It's user-friendly but knowing where everything is can save you a lot of time. Next, integrate Jasper with your existing tools. Whether you use WordPress for blogging or Mailchimp for email marketing, integrating Jasper can streamline your workflow, allowing you to send AI-generated content directly to these platforms.

Creating Content with Jasper

Now, let's create some content. Start by selecting the type of content you want to create. Jasper provides templates for various content types, which is handy, especially if you're juggling multiple formats. For instance, if you're crafting a blog post, choose the blog post template, which prompts you to input a title, keywords, and a brief description of the post. Jasper then takes this input and generates a draft for you. It's like sketching out a rough outline, which you can refine and expand. Here, you can leverage Jasper's capabilities by inputting prompts that guide the AI to produce the specific style and tone you want. Say you're targeting a young, vibrant audience; phrases like "latest trends," "must-try," or "pro tips" can steer Jasper in the right direction.

Advanced Features

As you get more comfortable with Jasper, begin exploring its advanced features. One of the standout features is the 'Boss Mode,' which allows you to take more control over the AI, directing it with specific commands. You can tell Jasper to "write a conclusion emphasizing the benefits of nuclear energy" or "create an intro that hooks the reader with a surprising statistic." This feature is particularly useful for creating content that needs to meet specific marketing goals or engage particular audience segments. Another advanced feature worth exploring is Jasper's SEO mode, which integrates with Surfer SEO to ensure that the content you create is reader-friendly and optimized for search engines. This is crucial if you're relying on organic search traffic for your blog or website, as it helps ensure that your content ranks well, drawing more visitors to your site.

Navigating through Jasper's array of features might seem daunting at first. Still, once you get the hang of it, you'll find it an indispensable tool in your content creation arsenal. The key to maximizing Jasper is experimenting with different prompts and settings to see what works best for your needs. Every piece of content has its demands, and with Jasper, you have the flexibility to meet these demands creatively and efficiently. Whether you're a seasoned content creator looking to streamline your workflow or a business owner needing to ramp up your content marketing efforts, Jasper offers a powerful way to enhance the quality and impact of your content.

3.3 Mastering GitHub Copilot for Code Generation

Are you a code writer, or do you want to be? Think of GitHub Copilot as your coding sidekick, always ready to toss in a useful code snippet or even craft entire functions for you on the fly. This tool is like having a highly experienced coder sitting beside you, constantly ready to suggest the best coding practices, shortcuts, and creative solutions to tricky problems. Developed as a collaboration between GitHub and

OpenAI, Copilot uses the power of an AI model trained on a plethora of code from public repositories on GitHub. This means it doesn't just understand code; it understands *how* coders code, making it an invaluable resource whether you're building a complex application or just dabbling in a new programming language.

Setting up GitHub Copilot is surprisingly straightforward. First, you'll need a GitHub account (github.com), a hub for millions of developers worldwide. Once you've got that sorted, installing Copilot involves adding it as an extension to your preferred code editor. GitHub has ensured that Copilot integrates smoothly with popular editors like Visual Studio Code. After installation, it seamlessly syncs into your coding environment, sitting discreetly in the corner, ready to jump in with suggestions the moment you start typing. The setup is designed to be non-intrusive, so it enhances your workflow without disrupting it. Once Copilot is up and running, it offers suggestions in real-time, right in the line of code you're working on, much like how a predictive text feature works on your smartphone, but much more sophisticated.

Using GitHub Copilot effectively can significantly enhance your coding efficiency and improve the quality of your code. The key is interacting with it as a collaborative tool rather than just an autocomplete function. For instance, when you start typing a function, Copilot doesn't just passively suggest completions—it actively offers entire blocks of code that can be instantly integrated into your project. This can be particularly handy when dealing with more formulaic code structures, like setting up API calls or configuring new services in your application. By customizing your interactions with Copilot, such as adjusting the specificity of the code it generates, you can tailor its outputs to be more aligned with your coding style and the requirements of your project.

However, while Copilot can be a tremendous asset, it's important to approach it with a critical eye. This brings us to the ethical considerations and best practices in using such a powerful tool. One of the foremost concerns is the integrity of the code it suggests. Since Copilot learns from publicly available code, not all suggestions are guaranteed optimal or even entirely secure. It's crucial, therefore, to review each piece of code Copilot generates and understand its function and impact on your overall project before integration. This ensures your codebase remains robust and helps avoid inadvertently introducing security flaws or bugs into your application.

Moreover, relying too heavily on Copilot for code generation could lead to missed learning opportunities, particularly for those new to coding. While it's tempting to let an AI handle the complexities of coding, there's immense value in understanding the logic and structure of your code firsthand. Therefore, Copilot should be used as a learning tool as much as a coding assistant. Try to understand why it suggests specific codes and explore alternative solutions it might offer. This way, you get your project done more efficiently and enhance your coding skills progressively.

In essence, GitHub Copilot represents a significant leap forward in software development. It exemplifies how AI can be leveraged to automate tasks and enhance human capabilities and creativity. As you continue integrating Copilot into your coding practices, remember to balance leveraging AI assistance and nurturing your own coding skills. With the right approach, Copilot can transform how you code, making the process faster, more efficient, and, surprisingly, more educational.

3.4 THE ULTIMATE GUIDE TO CREATING PROMPTS FOR GENERATIVE AI

First, a "prompt" is simply a sentence that gives the AI instructions on what you want it to create or research. Crafting the perfect prompt for a generative AI might seem simple, but there's real art to doing it well. When aiming to get the most creative and relevant outputs from an AI, how you phrase your prompts can make a significant difference. Let's break down the basics of crafting effective prompts. It's all about being precise, specific, and intentional. Think of it as giving directions to someone who's never visited your city. You wouldn't just say, "Go downtown." Instead, you'd provide specific streets or landmarks. Similarly, with AI, the more exact your prompt, the better the AI can navigate its vast learning and deliver precisely what you're looking for.

For instance, a vague prompt like "write a product description" will yield generic results if you use an AI to generate marketing copy. However, refining your prompt to "write a 100-word product description for a luxury skincare cream targeted at women aged 30-40 who enjoy organic products" guides the AI much more effectively. This specificity helps the AI understand what to write and the style and nuances appropriate for the target audience. The principle here is precision. You're setting parameters allowing the AI to understand the scope and context of what's needed, making generating relevant and high-quality content easier.

Moving on to prompt engineering techniques, these are your next-level strategies to home in on those AI outputs. Advanced techniques involve layering your prompts with specificity, context, and potential use cases. Let's say you're working on a script for a video tutorial about gardening. Instead of a simple command like "create a script," try layering in details about the audience, the key message, and even the tone. A prompt like, "Create an engaging and informative script for a 10-minute video tutorial on urban gardening for beginners, using a friendly and encouraging tone," gives the AI a clear direction and an understanding of the desired outcome.

This approach can significantly enhance the relevance of the AI's outputs, making them more tailored and ready for use. It's like fine-tuning a musical instrument; the better you calibrate it, the better it performs.

What do you do when AI doesn't produce the expected results? Troubleshooting common issues in AI-generated content often comes back to refining your prompts. If the output is off the mark, revisit your prompt and adjust it for clarity or specificity. Sometimes, it's a matter of adding more context or using different terminology that the model might recognize better. For instance, if an AI-generated recipe keeps using the wrong type of ingredient, you might need to specify "use fresh ingredients only" to steer it correctly.

Remember, working with generative AI is a dynamic process. Each interaction is an opportunity to refine and improve your prompts, enhancing the AI's ability to produce valuable and creative outputs. Whether you're crafting narratives, developing marketing content, or generating technical articles, the power of a well-crafted prompt is undeniable. It's your key to unlocking the full potential of AI in your writing, ensuring that every piece of content is not just created but crafted with precision and purpose.

Try these two prompts in your ChatGPT account to see the difference:

- "Write a short video script on gardening."
- "Create an engaging and informative script for a 1-minute video tutorial on urban gardening for beginners, using a friendly and encouraging tone."

3.5 FROM SIMPLE TO COMPLEX: CRAFTING ADVANCED AI PROMPTS

When you begin to think about using AI for more than just generating straightforward responses, you enter a realm where the intricacies of AI's interpretative skills come into play. Understanding how different AI models interpret and respond to prompts is a game-changer. AI operates on a mechanism that parses through the input data (your prompts) and searches its vast database for patterns and correlations that match this input. This means the more detailed and layered your prompts are, the more effectively AI can dig through its training to generate sophisticated outputs.

For instance, if you're working on a project that requires the AI to generate technical descriptions of advanced machinery, simply asking the AI to describe a machine" won't suffice. You'll need to specify the type of machine, its use, key features, and the intended audience for this description. You might try instead prompting the AI "Describe a Pixma Pro-200, an efficient color ink printer that prints high-speed photos. Make the description a sales promotion to sell the printer to photographers." This detailed prompt helps the AI understand more explicitly what you're asking for and the context in which the information will be used, significantly impacting the relevance and accuracy of the content it generates.

The goal is to leverage the AI's capabilities to handle complex tasks by crafting prompts that guide the AI in a very pointed direction. This could involve layering your prompts with multiple questions, each building on the last, to guide the AI through a logical sequence of thought or to embed specific keywords that trigger the AI's recognition patterns towards a particular type of response. For example, when seeking creative content, using evocative language in your prompts can stir the AI towards more imaginative outputs. Phrases like "envision a scenario where..." or "imagine if..." signal the AI to switch from a purely informational mode to a more creative one. Also, when creating your prompts, you can use bullet points and a sentence to give the AI additional parameters you'd like it to understand.

Interactive prompting is another fascinating area. This involves engaging in a dialogue with the AI, where you refine its outputs iteratively. Think of it as sculpting; with each exchange, you chip away the excess, gradually honing in on your desired form. You might start with a broad prompt, review the output, and then ask follow-up questions based on the initial response to refine the concept further.

This method is particularly useful when working on complex projects where the first response only meets some of the requirements. It's a dynamic way to use AI, turning it into a truly interactive tool that can adapt and evolve in response to your inputs. Think of it in terms of giving further instructions to your assistant to refine what you're looking for in the response.

Exploring the creative applications of advanced prompts opens up many possibilities across various fields. For example, advanced prompts can create highly targeted marketing advertising campaigns. By incorporating demographic data into your prompts, AI can generate content that resonates with specific audience segments, increasing engagement and effectiveness. In education, sophisticated prompts can help develop comprehensive learning modules tailored to the needs of different learning styles. The AI can be prompted to present the same information in various formats—textual, auditory, or visual—making learning more accessible to everyone.

As you move forward with using AI in your creative or technical projects, remember that the sophistication of your prompts plays a crucial role in the quality of the outputs you receive. By understanding and leveraging AI's response mechanisms and experimenting with complex prompt designs and interactive prompting, you can enhance your ability to use AI as a powerful tool for innovation and creativity.

You used ChatGPT to generate a short video script in the previous section. Once you've done that, tell ChatGPT this to see what I mean about refining prompts and being interactive:

- "Include specific details on growing tomatoes."

In wrapping up this exploration into the art of crafting advanced AI prompts, it's clear that the potential applications are as vast as your imagination allows them to be. With a solid grasp of effectively communicating with AI, you're well-equipped to push the boundaries of what's possible in writing, coding, content creation, or any other field where AI can lend its capabilities. As we transition into the next chapter, we'll delve deeper into how AI is reshaping specific industries, providing you with insights and strategies to leverage AI for professional growth and innovation. The journey through AI's capabilities is just beginning, and the tools and techniques discussed here are your map and compass for navigating the exciting terrain ahead.

CHAPTER 4:
GENERATIVE AI FOR VISUAL CREATIVES

Have you ever found yourself staring at a blank canvas or screen, wishing you could describe what you envision and see it come to life? Well, that's not wishful thinking anymore; it's possible with DALL·E. This incredible AI technology turns textual descriptions into detailed images, making it a groundbreaking tool for artists, marketers, and anyone who wants to visualize ideas without needing to pick up a brush or master complex design software. Imagine typing "a two-tiered chocolate cake under a bright disco light" and getting a vibrant, detailed image of precisely that. Welcome to the world of creating with DALL·E, where your words set the visual scene.

4.1 AN INTRODUCTION TO CREATING WITH DALL·E

Getting to Know DALL·E: Overview of DALL·E's Capabilities in Generating Visual Content from Textual Descriptions (openart.ai to open an account)

DALL·E, developed by OpenAI, is not your ordinary AI; it's a specialized model capable of generating unique, high-quality images from plain text descriptions. This capability is not just about creating random illustrations; DALL·E understands and interprets the components of your descriptions with astonishing nuance. For instance, if you describe a scene as "a sunny day at the beach with a dog playing frisbee," DALL·E doesn't just generate any beach scene; it carefully incorporates all specified elements to reflect the sunny setting, the playful dog, and the motion of a frisbee. This level of detail and accuracy makes DALL·E an invaluable tool for creators who need quick visualizations of their ideas or want to explore creative concepts with limited resources.

Setting Up for Success: Tips for Preparing Effective Prompts and Utilizing DALL·E's Interface

Communicating your vision through prompts is the key to getting the most out of DALL·E. Crafting an effective prompt goes beyond just describing an object or scene; it involves being specific about styles, emotions, and even the composition of your desired image. For example, instead of "a cat," say "a fluffy white cat with emerald eyes sitting on a sunny windowsill." Such precision guides DALL·E in generating images more aligned with your specific needs. When you start using DALL·E, take some time to familiarize yourself with its interface. The platform is user-friendly, but knowing where to tweak settings like image resolution or style can significantly enhance your output quality.

Creative Explorations with DALL·E: Examples of Creative Projects and Visual Experiments Facilitated by DALL·E

The potential for creative projects with DALL·E is boundless. Artists have used it to conceptualize surreal landscapes that combine elements from different ecosystems, creating fantastical scenes that could inspire stories or video games. Marketers have leveraged DALL·E to generate images for campaigns requiring a quick turnaround, ensuring fresh and visually engaging content. Educators use DALL·E to bring historical events to life for students through compelling visualizations that depict detailed reconstructions of historical settings, making learning more interactive and enjoyable.

Navigating Legal and Ethical Considerations: Discussion on Copyright, Ethics, and Responsible Use of AI-Generated Images

While DALL·E opens up a world of creative possibilities, it also brings important legal and ethical considerations to the forefront. The ease of creating detailed images can tempt one to reproduce copyrighted characters or artworks. Still, it's crucial to navigate these waters carefully. Always ensure that the images you generate and use do not infringe on existing copyrights, particularly if you plan to use them commercially. Additionally, consider the ethical implications of AI-generated art: when does it enhance creativity, and when could it potentially undermine human artists? Awareness of these factors helps maintain the responsible use of AI technologies like DALL·E, ensuring they foster creativity and innovation without crossing ethical boundaries.

Using DALL·E, you're no longer just a creator but a visionary who can bring fantastical ideas to visual reality at the speed of thought. As you continue experimenting and creating with DALL·E, remember that each prompt is a brushstroke in your ever-expanding canvas of possibilities.

4.2 USING AI TO DESIGN LOGOS AND BRANDING MATERIALS

Imagine stepping into branding, where every color, shape, and font choice tells a part of your business's story. Think about mixing this creative process with AI's computational power and data-driven insights. That's where AI-powered design tools come into play, revolutionizing how logos and branding materials are created. These tools aren't just about automating design tasks; they're about enhancing the creative process, providing you with endless creativity and precision. Tools like Looka and Brandmark use AI to understand your brand's ethos and aesthetics and suggest logo designs that reflect your company's identity. What's fascinating here is how these tools adapt to user feedback, evolving their suggestions to match your vision with each iteration better. It's like having a design assistant who instantly learns from your preferences and continuously improves the suggestions.

Creating logos and branding materials with AI is streamlined yet detailed. It starts with you inputting basic information about your brand, such as your company name, industry, and any tagline you use. Then, you might be asked to describe your brand's personality— Is it conservative or bold? Luxurious or economical? Describing specifics helps the AI grasp what you're looking for. Following this, AI tools typically present a selection of styles, fonts, and color schemes. You pick what resonates most, and the AI uses your choices to generate several logo options. From here, you can further tweak the designs, adjusting elements like the color palette or the font style until you find the perfect match that embodies your brand's identity. This method isn't just about getting a new logo; it's about crafting a visual identity that tells your brand's story at a glance.

When it comes to customization and refinement, AI tools offer remarkable flexibility. They allow you to fine-tune designs to ensure that the final product isn't just visually appealing and aligns perfectly with your brand's messaging. Adjusting a font's thickness, the color gradient, or the spacing between symbols can drastically influence the perception of your brand. AI's ability to simulate and instantly show the impact of these changes allows you to experiment with different aesthetics without committing to costly prototypes. This iterative process supported by AI ensures that the final design stands out visually and resonates with your target audience, enhancing brand recognition and loyalty.

In this ever-evolving landscape of brand development, AI design tools are not just about keeping up with the latest trends; they're about setting new benchmarks in creativity and efficiency. They provide a space where data meets design, where every choice is informed yet imaginative, allowing brands to craft an identity that's beautiful and strategically poised for success. As you continue exploring AI's potential in your branding efforts, remember that each tool offers unique features that can be tailored to meet your specific needs, ensuring that your brand's story is not just told but vibrantly showcased.

4.3 AI AND ANIMATION: A MATCH MADE IN DIGITAL HEAVEN

The animation industry, known for its intense labor and time-consuming processes, is undergoing a transformative shift thanks to AI's integration into various stages of production. From breathing life into characters to refining complex animation sequences, AI is not just streamlining workflows but also enhancing creative freedom, allowing animators to push the boundaries of traditional storytelling. Imagine a world where characters in animations can evolve in response to audience emotions or intricate animation sequences can be refined in real-time, enhancing the viewer's experience. That's the kind of innovation AI is bringing to the table.

AI's role in character design and motion capture is particularly revolutionary. Traditionally, character design has been a meticulous process where artists sketch numerous iterations, and motion capture involves actors donning suits dotted with sensors to record movements. However, AI is changing the game by automating parts of these processes and adding layers of efficiency. For instance, AI can now analyze thousands of human expressions and movements to automatically generate a range of character animations that animators can further customize. This speeds up the animation process and ensures a level of detail that might be too subtle or complex for human animators to capture consistently.

Moreover, AI's capability in motion capture is advancing to a point where it can translate even the most minor nuances of an actor's performance into digital characters in real time without the need for cumbersome suits or extensive post-processing. This technology uses machine learning algorithms trained on countless hours of video, teaching the system to recognize and predict human movements with high precision. This development is particularly exciting for projects that require complex emotional performances or detailed action sequences, as it allows for more dynamic and expressive animations that genuinely capture the essence of the performance.

Tools and Techniques: Introduction to Accessible AI Tools and Techniques for Animators at All Skill Levels

In animation, AI tools and techniques are becoming more accessible, enabling a broader range of creatives to harness these advancements. Software like Adobe Character Animator and Autodesk Maya incorporates AI-driven tools that automate critical aspects of the animation process, such as lip-syncing and facial expressions, based on voice and video inputs. These tools are designed with user-friendly interfaces that lower the entry barrier for emerging animators and small studios, allowing them to produce high-quality animations without requiring extensive resources.

Beyond mainstream software, there are specialized AI tools that cater to more specific animation needs. For example, RunwayML offers capabilities that allow animators to apply machine learning models directly to their animation projects, enabling features like style transfer, where the visual style of one image can be applied to another, or pose estimation, which can be used to animate 2D characters based on video footage of real people. These tools are powerful and customizable, giving animators the flexibility to tweak AI settings to fit the specific needs of their projects.

Collaborating with AI: Strategies for Effectively Integrating AI into the Creative Process of Animation

Integrating AI into the creative process requires a balanced approach that respects both the technological capabilities and the artistic vision. One effective strategy is to use AI as a collaborative partner that can take on repetitive or data-intensive tasks, freeing up human artists to focus on the more creative aspects of animation. For instance, AI can generate multiple scene variations, which the creative team can then review and refine, ensuring that the final output is both efficient and creatively fulfilling.

Another strategy involves iterative feedback loops where AI suggestions are continuously refined based on human input. This collaborative process allows AI to learn from the artistic decisions of human animators, improving over time to better align with the team's creative goals. Such an approach not only enhances the efficiency of the animation process but also ensures that the technology supports rather than dictates the creative vision.

Future Trends: Speculation on Future Developments in AI-Assisted Animation and Storytelling

Looking to the future, the potential developments in AI-assisted animation and storytelling are boundless. We are likely to see AI becoming more intuitive and capable of making creative decisions, suggesting plot developments or character arcs based on narrative data it has analyzed. This could lead to a new era of storytelling where AI and humans co-create stories that dynamically adapt to audience reactions in real time. Imagine going to a movie three times and each time it has differences.

Furthermore, as virtual reality and augmented reality continue to grow, AI-driven animation will be crucial in creating more immersive and interactive experiences. Imagine VR movies where the storyline and characters adapt based on the viewer's interactions, all rendered in real-time with lifelike animations powered by AI. This represents a significant shift in how stories are told and experienced and opens up exciting new opportunities for creative expression and audience engagement.

As you continue to explore the fascinating intersection of AI and animation, remember that these tools are here to amplify your creative potential, not replace it. They offer new ways to imagine, create, and inspire, transforming the art of animation into a more dynamic and inclusive craft.

4.4 AIVA FOR MUSIC COMPOSITION: UNLEASHING YOUR INNER BEETHOVEN (AIVA.AI FOR FREE ACCOUNT)

If you've ever dreamed of composing music that stirs the soul but felt held back by your lack of formal training, AIVA (Artificial Intelligence Virtual Artist) could be your gateway to unlocking musical creativity. AIVA is a cutting-edge AI specifically designed to compose music. It's been trained on the works of classical composers like Bach and Mozart, enabling it to produce compositions that resonate with the depth and complexity you'd expect from a seasoned musician. This isn't just about robotic tunes; AIVA creates music that can evoke emotions, build atmospheres, and even tell stories, all through the mathematical precision of AI.

Starting a project with AIVA is like partnering with a virtual Beethoven. First, you'll need to define the type of music you want to create. Are you looking for a stirring symphony, a jazz piece, or a modern pop sound? Your input guides AIVA's output, so the more precise your vision, the better the results. Once you've set your musical genre, you can dive deeper into the nuances—decide on the piece's mood, the instruments involved, and even the tempo. AIVA offers a user-friendly interface where you can input these preferences. Here's a pro tip: Consider each setting an ingredient in a recipe, and the more precise your ingredients are, the more delightful the meal—or, in this case, the music.

As you move from setup to actual composition, AIVA begins to weave its magic. Using its vast database of musical knowledge, it starts crafting melodies line by line, harmonizing them with accompanying chords and rhythms. What's fascinating is how AIVA applies complex musical theories and patterns learned from centuries of music to create something entirely new and unique. You can generate a complete composition in minutes, which might take a human composer days or weeks to achieve. This rapid turnaround is impressive and incredibly inspiring, especially for those who thrive on instant feedback and iteration.

However, every AI-generated piece is a starting point, not the final say. Personalizing AIVA's creations involves a bit of back-and-forth, like editing a draft in writing. Adjust the tempo, change a few notes in the melody, or switch out instruments to see how they alter the piece's feel. This part of the process is crucial because it melds your personal touch with AIVA's computational creativity. It's about molding the AI's output to align with your creative vision, ensuring the music sounds good and feels right to you, reflecting your emotional and artistic intentions.

Navigating the complexities of copyright with AI-composed music adds another layer of consideration. When you create music using AIVA, who exactly holds the copyright? Generally, the copyright would belong to you as the composer using the tool, similar to using a musical instrument to create a piece. However, the landscape is evolving, and it's vital to stay informed about current laws and regulations, which can vary by country. Ensuring your compositions are legally compliant protects your creative rights. It respects the intellectual property laws designed to foster innovation and creativity across industries.

Remember that tools like AIVA are here to enhance your creative capabilities, allowing you to explore musical landscapes that might otherwise remain out of reach. Whether you're a seasoned musician looking to experiment with new styles or a newcomer eager to express yourself through music, AIVA offers a platform to expand your creative horizons.

In this chapter, we've seen how AI like DALL·E, branding tools, and AIVA are not just tools but collaborators that bring your creative visions to life in visual and musical forms. They democratize creativity, making sophisticated art and music composition accessible to everyone.

CHAPTER 5:
VOICE AND AUDIO APPLICATIONS

Imagine conversing with someone who sounds convincingly human, but it's an AI voice. From soothing narrators in audiobooks to dynamic characters in video games, the voices you hear are increasingly powered by AI. This isn't science fiction—it's the reality of voice generation technology today. This chapter peels back the curtain on how synthetic voices are created, tailored, and brought into play across various sectors, transforming how we interact with technology daily. It's like having the ultimate vocal chameleon at your fingertips, ready to adapt to whatever task you have in mind.

5.1 THE BASICS OF VOICE GENERATION WITH AI

Understanding AI Voice Generation: An Introduction to the Technology Behind Synthetic Voice Creation

The magic behind AI voice generation lies in its ability to mimic human speech patterns so closely that it's often hard to tell the difference. But how does it work? At its core, voice generation technology uses a branch of AI known as text-to-speech (TTS) to convert written text into spoken words. This process involves two main stages: text analysis and sound production. During text analysis, the AI breaks down the text into phonetic components, understanding the nuances of language, from syntax to emotion. Then, in the sound production stage, these phonetic components are converted into audio output replicating human speech, complete with intonation, rhythm, and emotion.

To achieve this, AI systems are trained on vast datasets of human speech, learning various speech patterns, accents, and tones. This training allows them to generate voice outputs that are incredibly lifelike. Advanced voice synthesis models like Google's WaveNet have taken this a step further by using deep neural networks to produce voices that can laugh, cry, and shout, providing a richer audio experience that can engage and resonate with users on a deeper level.

Choosing the Right Tool: Guidance on Selecting AI Voice Generation Tools Based on Project Needs

Selecting the right AI voice-generation tool can be pivotal in determining the success of your project. Whether you're developing an interactive game, creating a virtual assistant, or producing an audiobook, the quality of the voice output can make a significant difference. When choosing a tool, consider factors such as the naturalness of the voice, the languages and dialects supported, customization capabilities, and ease of integration with other software.

Tools like Amazon Polly and IBM Watson offer extensive customization options and support multiple languages, making them suitable for global applications. Meanwhile, tools like Descript are tailored for content creators, providing features that allow for easy editing and manipulation of voice recordings. ElevenLabs, Murf.ai, and Amazon KDP's Virtual Voice are popular options in the AI voice technology audiobook market today. By aligning the tool's capabilities with your project's specific needs, you can ensure a more seamless and effective implementation of voice technology.

Creating Your First AI Voice: Step-by-step Process for Generating a Synthetic Voice, from Selecting Voice Attributes to Output

Creating your first AI voice can be an exciting venture. Start by defining the character or role of your AI voice. Is it a friendly travel guide, a knowledgeable tutor, or a charismatic storyteller? This will guide your decisions regarding the voice's age, gender, tone, and style. Next, select a voice generation tool that suits your project's needs and budget. Once you've chosen a tool, the next step is to input your script or text. This is where you can specify the emotional tone or specific pronunciation instructions.

Most AI voice tools offer a preview function, allowing you to listen to how the voice sounds with your text. Use this feature to adjust the pacing, pitch, or emphasis to better match your vision. Once you're satisfied with the settings, you can generate the voice output. This output can then be integrated into your project, whether a digital ad, an educational video, or an interactive application, adding a layer of engagement through human-like speech.

Applications and Use Cases: Exploring the Diverse Applications of AI-generated Voices in Media, Entertainment, and Customer Service

The applications of AI-generated voices are as diverse as they are transformative. In the media industry, synthetic voices are used to produce weather reports and news updates, allowing for real-time broadcasting without the need for constant human input. In entertainment, video games use AI voices to bring characters to life, offering players a more immersive and interactive experience.

One of the most impactful applications is in customer service. AI-powered voice assistants can simultaneously handle a high volume of inquiries, providing instant customer responses. This not only enhances customer satisfaction but also optimizes operational efficiency. For instance, a virtual customer service agent can guide a user through troubleshooting steps, manage booking inquiries, or provide product recommendations, all in a friendly and conversational tone.

These applications showcase just a fraction of what's possible with AI voice technology. As we continue to innovate and integrate these tools into various fields, the potential to enhance and personalize user experiences through the power of voice is boundless. Whether through storytelling, customer interaction, or content creation, synthetic voices are reshaping the auditory landscape, offering new ways to engage, inform, and entertain.

5.2 PODCASTING MADE EASY WITH AI

Podcasting has exploded in popularity, becoming an essential medium for storytelling, education, and entertainment. However, the production process can be daunting, involving several stages from initial planning to final editing. This is where AI steps in, revolutionizing how podcasts are created, edited, and distributed, making it easier for you to focus on what truly matters—creating engaging content for your audience.

AI in podcast production is like having a multitasking wizard by your side. It simplifies the entire production process, from the conceptual stage to post-production. Imagine the early stages of planning a podcast episode. Typically, you'd spend hours researching topics, scripting, and organizing content. AI can streamline these tasks by helping you gather and process information faster. AI-powered tools can scour the internet for trending topics, suggest fresh content ideas based on listener preferences, and even help outline your episodes. This can significantly cut down your preparation time, allowing you to produce content more consistently.

Once you move into the recording phase, AI plays a crucial role. For instance, voice-controlled AI can manage your recording equipment, adjust levels, and even handle the recording through simple voice commands. This integration makes the technical aspects of podcasting more accessible to beginners and reduce the workload for solo podcasters who manage all aspects of production. Editing, which is often the most time-consuming part of podcast production, AI tools are a game-changer. They can automatically cut out silences, balance sound levels, and even remove ums and ahs. This speeds up the editing process and ensures a polished final product that sounds professional.

Content creation with AI in podcasting isn't just about streamlining production; it's also about enhancing the quality of the content. AI can generate scripts for your episodes based on crucial points you input, ensuring your content is cohesive and engaging. It can help draft show notes that are clear and informative, providing valuable resources for your listeners. Perhaps more impressively, AI can even participate in hosting. AI hosts can interact with human hosts in episodes, provide factual information, or narrate portions of content. This can add a unique dynamic to your podcast, making it more interactive and diverse.

AI's capabilities in enhancing audio quality are impressive. Sophisticated AI algorithms can improve sound quality by reducing background noise, optimizing speech clarity, and adjusting the audio for various platforms, ensuring your podcast sounds great, whether played on a car stereo, smartphone, or high-end headphones. This level of audio enhancement was once only possible with professional audio engineering skills. Still, AI puts these capabilities in the hands of every podcaster, ensuring that you can produce studio-quality sound from your home or office.

The role of AI continues once the podcast is ready to go live. AI tools also assist in the distribution and analysis of your podcast. They can optimize the release timings based on when your audience is most likely to listen, auto-publish episodes across multiple platforms, and even help you manage promotions across social networks. After your podcast is out in the world, AI-driven analytics tools can track who is listening, from where, and on what devices. It can even gauge how listeners respond to different parts of each episode. This data is crucial as it helps you better understand your audience, allowing you to tailor future content to meet their preferences and grow your listener base more effectively.

Incorporating AI into your podcast production can transform a complex, time-consuming process into something more manageable and enjoyable. It allows you to consistently produce high-quality, engaging content, giving you the edge in a highly competitive space. Whether you're a newcomer eager to make your mark or a seasoned podcaster looking to optimize your workflow, AI tools offer both the simplicity to get you started and the depth to scale up your productions. As we continue to explore AI's evolving role in media production, its impact on podcasting remains a compelling testament to its potential to democratize content creation, making high-quality podcasting achievable for creators everywhere.

5.3 CREATING CUSTOM AUDIO BOOKS WITH GENERATIVE AI

The audiobook market has seen a phenomenal rise in popularity, thanks partly to their convenience and immersive experience. But a new player is changing the game even further: AI narration. This technology is reshaping how audiobooks are produced, offering a range of voices and styles that can be tailored to any text, making books more accessible and engaging than ever before. Imagine having the ability to choose a narrator's tone, pace, and even emotional expression explicitly tailored for the book's content. That's the level of customization AI brings to audiobook production.

When you dive into producing an audiobook with AI, the first step is to select the right narration style. This choice can dramatically affect how listeners perceive and engage with the content. You might opt for a warm, friendly voice for a personal development book or a suspenseful tone for a thriller. AI tools provide a variety of preset styles, but many also allow for deeper customization. You can adjust specific aspects like pitch, speed, and timbre to create a voice that fits the narrative perfectly. Some platforms even offer the ability to modulate emotional tones across different parts of the book, which can help deliver a more dynamic listening experience.

Once you have selected the style and customized the voice, the next step is to produce the audio. This process is remarkably streamlined with AI. You feed the text into the AI system, and it converts it into speech in the chosen voice and style. But it's not just about converting text to speech. The AI also handles complex requirements like pronunciation corrections, pauses for effect, and emphasis on key phrases, which are crucial for maintaining the listener's engagement. One of the most powerful aspects of using AI in audiobook production is the ability to edit and tailor narration on the fly. It allows for a level of polish that can rival professionally recorded audiobooks but at a fraction of the time and cost.

Personalization and accessibility are perhaps the most significant advantages of AI-generated audiobooks. These technologies enable catering to a diverse range of listening preferences and needs. For instance, listeners with visual impairments or reading disabilities can benefit greatly from customized audiobooks tailored to the content and delivering that content. AI can adjust the speaking rate, enhance diction, or even alter the language to suit specific listener requirements. Furthermore, personalization isn't limited to physical or educational needs. Imagine a scenario where you prefer to listen to all your books in a particular voice or accent. AI makes it possible to recreate the same voice across different books, providing a consistent listening experience uniquely suited to your preferences.

Navigating the copyright and ethical considerations in AI audiobook production is crucial. As you employ AI to voice human-written texts, it's essential to ensure that the usage rights of the text are clear, and that the production complies with all relevant laws. This includes obtaining the necessary permissions to use the text and ensuring that the AI's voice does not infringe on the rights of human voice actors. Ethical considerations also come into play, particularly in terms of transparency. Listeners should be aware that they are listening to an AI-generated voice. This transparency not only ensures ethical clarity but also helps in setting the right expectations for the audience.

As we move forward, integrating AI in audiobook production will redefine the norms of publishing and listening. It creates a world where books are more accessible, production is more efficient, and listener experiences can be highly personalized. As these technologies continue to evolve and improve, the future of audiobooks looks more vibrant and accessible than ever, promising a new era where everyone can have a tailored listening experience that meets their individual needs and preferences.

CHAPTER 6:
AI-ENHANCED BUSINESS STRATEGIES

Stepping into the business world isn't just about having a groundbreaking idea; it's about effectively planning, analyzing, and executing strategies that transform that idea into reality. Now, imagine if you had a powerhouse tool that could handle heaps of data, crunch numbers at lightning speed, and provide insights that are not just fast but incredibly accurate. Welcome to the AI era, where AI is your ultimate business strategist, enhancing every facet of your business planning and execution. This isn't about replacing the human touch in business; it's about augmenting your capabilities to plan better, predict smarter, and perform stronger.

6.1 CRAFTING A BUSINESS PLAN WITH AI

Automating Market Analysis

Diving into market analysis traditionally involves sifting through mountains of data, consumer surveys, and industry reports—a process that's both time-consuming and prone to human error. But with AI, you can automate this entire process. AI tools are designed to scan extensive datasets, identify trends, and even predict market shifts before they become apparent. Imagine having a system that not only gathers all this data but also analyzes and customizes it to highlight personalized opportunities and threats without you having to comb through spreadsheet after spreadsheet. This level of automation allows you to focus more on strategy and less on legwork, ensuring your decisions are informed by the most comprehensive and up-to-date information available.

Financial Projections and Forecasts

When it comes to financial planning, precision is key. AI transforms historical data and current market dynamics into reliable financial forecasts. By employing sophisticated algorithms, AI can simulate various financial scenarios based on differing market conditions, giving you a clearer picture of potential risks and returns. This isn't just about seeing numbers; it's about understanding potential financial outcomes and preparing for them effectively. Whether you're planning your budget, forecasting sales, or assessing investment returns, AI provides depth and precision that traditional methods cannot match.

Competitive Landscape Analysis

Understanding your competition is crucial, and AI can provide this competitive edge. AI systems can continually monitor your competitors' online presence, from social media buzz to online customer reviews, and provide real-time insights into their strategies and customer sentiments. This ongoing analysis helps you identify what your competitors are doing right or wrong and uncovers gaps in the market that you can capitalize on. By leveraging AI, you can stay ahead, adapting your strategies dynamically to maintain a competitive advantage in a fast-paced market.

Streamlining Business Plan Documentation

Lastly, let's tackle the often-tedious task of business plan documentation. AI can help streamline the creation and refinement of your business plans. With AI-driven text generation tools, you can automate parts of the document creation, such as executive summaries or market analysis sections. These tools are designed to generate coherent and professionally phrased content based on your inputs, ensuring that your business plan isn't just thorough and well-articulated. AI can suggest enhancements in your plan's language and structure, refining and honing your plan, making the entire process more efficient and effective.

Incorporating AI into your business strategy isn't just about keeping up with technology—it's about setting a foundation that allows you to innovate, predict, and execute with a level of precision and foresight that was previously unreachable. As you integrate these AI tools into your planning and analysis, you're not just optimizing your processes; you're transforming them, ensuring that every decision is data-driven, every strategy is informed, and every outcome is as successful as possible.

There are several AI platforms that you can use in your business, offering a range of tools from predictive analytics to financial forecasting and risk assessment. Here are three widely recognized AI platforms that could be particularly useful:

1. IBM Watson:

    - Features: IBM Watson provides advanced AI tools that can be applied to financial data to generate deep insights and predictions. It includes features for data visualization, predictive analytics, and natural language processing, which can help analyze financial trends, customer sentiment, and more.

    - Use Case: Ideal for businesses looking for robust AI capabilities to integrate into their existing systems, Watson can assist in areas like credit risk analysis and personalized financial advice.

2. Microsoft Azure AI:

- Features: Azure AI offers a comprehensive suite of machine learning tools and algorithms that can help in forecasting, anomaly detection, and financial modeling. Its cloud-based nature allows for scalability and integration with other Microsoft products.

- Use Case: Suitable for businesses already using Microsoft products; it can be beneficial for real-time financial data analysis and building custom financial models.

3. Google Cloud AI:

- Features: Google Cloud AI provides robust machine learning services and solutions that can be applied to financial analysis. Features include AI-driven demand forecasting, risk management tools, and investment predictions.

- Use Case: Good for businesses that need scalable and highly customizable AI tools; Google Cloud AI can help optimize investment portfolios and detect fraudulent financial activities.

These platforms offer different strengths and integration capabilities, so the best choice will depend on your specific business needs, existing infrastructure, and budget.

6.2 CHATBOTS FOR ENHANCED CUSTOMER ENGAGEMENT

Implementing AI chatbots into your customer service channels is like setting up a team of super-efficient, never-tiring support agents ready to engage with your customers 24/7. The beauty of AI chatbots lies in their ability to handle many customer interactions simultaneously, from answering FAQs to processing transactions and even providing personalized recommendations. Getting started with AI chatbots involves selecting a platform that aligns with your business needs–

handling customer inquiries, booking appointments, or providing technical support. Once you choose a platform, the next step is integrating it into your existing customer service framework. This integration typically involves setting up the chatbot on your website or customer interaction platforms like social media pages and ensuring it's equipped with the initial responses.

Training your chatbot is crucial. It begins with feeding it information about your products, services, and customer interaction scenarios. Over time, as it interacts with real customers, it learns and adapts, becoming more adept at handling complex queries about your business. Think of it as nurturing a new employee. Initially, you guide them through the processes, and gradually, they become more autonomous and skilled. The ongoing learning process is what makes AI chatbots particularly valuable. They analyze vast amounts of interaction data, learning from each conversation to improve their responses and actions. This capability allows them to offer highly personalized experiences to customers. For instance, if a customer frequently asks about a particular product feature, the chatbot can remember this preference and highlight related features or promotions in future interactions.

AI chatbots bring substantial operational efficiency. By automating routine inquiries and tasks, chatbots free up your human agents to focus on more complex and high-value interactions. This shift improves the efficiency of your customer service operations and reduces overall operational costs. Chatbots are tireless; they do not need breaks or vacations and can handle spikes in customer queries without additional resources. This reliability and efficiency make them indispensable, especially in handling after-hours queries or during high-traffic periods like sales or product launches.

Success Stories and Best Practices

Here are a couple of examples of how Chatbots have been used. One notable example comes from the hospitality sector. A renowned hotel chain implemented a chatbot with which guests could interact via smartphones. This chatbot handled everything from check-in and room service orders to providing local travel tips. The result was a significant increase in guest satisfaction as they enjoyed the convenience and promptness of service. Another success story is from the retail industry, where a famous clothing brand introduced a chatbot to help shoppers find products on their website. The chatbot provided personalized outfit recommendations based on the customer's style preferences and past purchases, increasing sales and customer engagement.

Best practices in implementing chatbots emphasize the importance of maintaining a human touch. Despite their efficiency, chatbots should only partially replace human interaction. Offering customers the option to speak with a human agent when the chatbot cannot resolve complex issues is crucial. It's also essential to continuously monitor and refine your chatbot's performance. Regularly updating the response database and adjusting the AI algorithms based on customer feedback ensures that the chatbot evolves in line with customer expectations and business changes. Additionally, being transparent with customers and letting them know they are interacting with a bot helps set the right expectations and fosters a trust-based relationship.

Incorporating AI chatbots into your business strategy transforms customer service operations into a more dynamic, efficient, and customer-friendly function.

Here are five AI chatbots that are widely used for customer service, along with their best use cases:

1. Microsoft Copilot Studios:

Copilot AI chatbot is very powerful and can be set up within minutes. If you want a chatbot that has all the information included on your business website, plus some internal FAQ documents, you can simply point the copilot chatbot at your website and give it the path to your internal documents. Through this "prompt" the copilot to learn from your site and your internal FAQs, and it's done. It will have the ability to generate the answer to any questions you may have about that information. Additionally, with a short 5-10 minutes you can publish your copilot chatbot, and your clientele will have immediate access.

2. Intercom:

- Use Case: Intercom is ideal for businesses that want to engage customers throughout their entire lifecycle. It supports real-time customer engagement, offers personalized conversation support, and is well-suited for handling inquiries and onboarding new users.

3. Zendesk Chat (formerly Zopim):

- Use Case: Zendesk Chat is best for companies requiring seamless integration with other customer service software. It excels at providing a unified agent interface with other Zendesk products, making it great for managing multi-channel customer support, including email, chat, and social media.

4. LivePerson:

- Use Case: This platform is particularly effective for enterprises looking for AI-driven messaging and automation capabilities. LivePerson allows businesses to automate responses and engage customers at scale on their preferred messaging channels, making it excellent for personalized customer interactions and marketing.

5. Drift:

- Use Case: Drift is perfect for businesses focused on increasing sales and generating leads via their website. It provides conversational marketing and sales tools that facilitate real-time sales assistance, qualifying leads directly through chat to accelerate the sales cycle.

Each of these chatbots is designed to enhance customer service by automating responses, managing inquiries, and providing personalized customer interactions. Depending on a business's specific needs, they shine in different aspects of customer engagement.

6.3 PREDICTING MARKET TRENDS WITH AI

Navigating the ever-evolving market landscape can feel like trying to catch smoke—it's there but fleeting and often elusive. That's where AI steps into the spotlight, not just as a tool but as a visionary partner that helps you see through the fog of data to predict the next big trends. Let's talk about how AI's capability to aggregate and analyze vast amounts of data transforms into actionable insights that can keep you ahead of the curve. Imagine having the ability to scan the global market environment, picking up on subtle shifts in consumer behavior, changes in economic indicators, or even social media sentiments, all in real time. AI integrates data from diverse sources and applies complex algorithms to identify patterns that might indicate emerging trends. This isn't just about having information; it's about understanding the context and the potential impacts of these trends on your business. It's like having a crystal ball, but instead of vague predictions, you get data-driven insights that can guide your strategic decisions.

But how does this play out in the real world? Consider how businesses in the fashion industry use AI to spot upcoming trends. By analyzing social media content, search trends, and online consumer behavior, AI tools can predict what colors, styles, or materials are gaining popularity. This allows designers and retailers to adjust their offerings proactively, aligning with consumer preferences even before they solidify into visible demand. Beyond fashion, in sectors like finance or healthcare, AI's ability to sift through economic reports, health data, or investment patterns helps businesses anticipate market demands or regulatory changes, significantly impacting their operational strategies and investment decisions.

Tools and Technologies

Diving deeper into the tools and technologies that make all this possible, we find many platforms designed to harness AI's predictive power. Platforms like IBM Watson and Google Cloud AI offer tools businesses can integrate to enhance their predictive analytics capabilities. These platforms use machine learning models that can be trained on specific data sets, ensuring the insights are tailored to your unique market context. For example, IBM Watson's predictive analytics tools can analyze customer data to forecast buying behaviors, helping businesses tailor their marketing efforts to meet anticipated needs. Similarly, Google Cloud AI provides solutions that can predict everything from customer churn rates to the likelihood of late payments, helping businesses manage risk and enhance customer retention strategies.

Moreover, these technologies are becoming more accessible. You don't need a team of data scientists to start leveraging AI for market trend analysis. Many AI platforms now offer user-friendly interfaces and pre-built models you can customize. This democratization of technology means that small to medium-sized enterprises can also jump on the AI bandwagon, using predictive analytics to compete effectively with more prominent industry players.

Challenges and Solutions

Integrating AI into your market trend analysis has its challenges. One common hurdle is the quality and quantity of data available. AI models are only as good as the data they are trained on. Incomplete or biased data can lead to inaccurate predictions, which mislead rather than guide your business decisions. To combat this, investing in robust data collection and management practices is crucial.

Ensuring your data is comprehensive and representative of all market segments you serve helps train more accurate AI models.

Another challenge is the interpretability of AI predictions. Sometimes, AI models can be a black box, providing predictions without clear explanations. This can be problematic when you need to justify strategic decisions based on these predictions. To address this, you can use platforms that offer explainable AI capabilities, which provide predictions and explain the factors influencing these predictions. This transparency builds trust in AI-driven insights and facilitates more informed decision-making.

AI's role in predicting market trends is akin to having a forward-looking radar that continuously scans the horizon for signals of change. By integrating AI-driven predictive analytics into your business strategy, you equip yourself with the tools to respond to market changes and anticipate them, positioning your business to thrive in a dynamic market environment. The power of AI lies not just in the technology itself but in how you harness these insights to drive growth and innovation in your business endeavors.

6.4 AI-DRIVEN MARKETING STRATEGIES FOR EVERY BUSINESS

Content Creation and Curation

In the fast-paced realm of digital marketing, keeping your content fresh and engaging can sometimes feel like you're running a never-ending marathon. Here's where AI comes into play, not just keeping pace but accelerating your content creation and curation efforts to new heights. Imagine an AI tool that generates content and ensures that it resonates deeply with your target audience. This is not about churning out generic posts; it's about crafting messages that speak directly to the interests and needs of your audience. AI-driven content tools analyze user engagement data and market trends to suggest content topics and formats that will likely perform well. For instance, if your audience engages more with video content on how-to topics, AI tools can identify this pattern and recommend producing more tutorials in video format.

Moreover, AI excels in curating content across platforms, ensuring that your brand maintains a consistent voice and style, whether posting on Instagram, tweeting, or updating your blog. This consistency builds a stronger brand identity and helps foster trust and loyalty among your audience. The beauty of using AI in content curation lies in its ability to blend historical data with real-time analytics, allowing you to optimize your content strategy continuously. For example, suppose an AI tool notices a spike in engagement from a particular post type or topic. In that case, it can automatically adjust your content calendar to capitalize on this trend, keeping your marketing efforts agile and responsive to audience preferences.

Here are three AI-driven content creation platforms that can help you generate, optimize, and enhance various types of content:

1. OpenAI's GPT-3/4:

    - Features: This advanced natural language processing tool can generate text for various uses, from blog posts and articles to creative writing and code. It's particularly useful for creating high-quality written content at scale.

    - Best Use Case: Ideal for businesses needing to produce large volumes of written content quickly, such as marketing agencies, media companies, and content-heavy websites.

2. Canva's Magic Write:

    - Features: Integrated into the Canva design platform, Magic Write leverages AI to help users create text for designs, including social media posts, presentations, and marketing materials. It also suggests design elements based on the content generated.

- Best Use Case: Perfect for businesses and individuals who need to combine visual content creation with text, such as for social media graphics, promotional materials, and presentations.

3. Articoolo:

- Features: Articoolo uses AI to help users create or rewrite articles. It can generate concise articles from keywords, helping overcome writer's block and reduce content creation time.

- Best Use Case: Suitable for content creators, bloggers, and digital marketers who need quick drafts or ideas to develop content for blogs, websites, and newsletters.

These platforms can significantly streamline content creation, offering different functionalities tailored to specific content needs, from text generation to integrated text and graphic design.

Customer Segmentation and Targeting

Diving deeper into the capabilities of AI in marketing, customer segmentation, and targeting are areas where AI flexes its muscles. The traditional methods of segmenting customers often involve broad categories that overlook the nuanced differences in customer behaviors and preferences. AI changes the game by analyzing detailed data points from customer interactions to create micro-segments. These micro-segments enable you to tailor your marketing messages with incredible precision. For instance, AI can identify a segment of customers who prefer eco-friendly products and are most active in the evenings. Armed with this insight, you can craft personalized email campaigns highlighting your latest eco-friendly products, sent out in the evenings when these customers are most likely to engage.

This level of targeting not only improves the effectiveness of your campaigns but also enhances the customer experience. Each interaction feels more personal and relevant, increasing the likelihood of conversion. Additionally, AI's learning algorithms continuously refine these segments based on new data, ensuring your marketing strategies evolve with your customer base. This dynamic approach to segmentation and targeting keeps your marketing efforts current and competitive.

Here are three platforms that excel in customer segmentation and targeting as well as other business needs:

1. HubSpot CRM:

    - Features: HubSpot provides robust CRM capabilities combined with marketing, sales, and service software that helps manage customer interactions based on detailed customer data analysis. It's also known for its accessibility across businesses of all sizes and its user-friendly interface and allows the segmentation of contacts by lifecycle stage, demographics, interaction history, and more.

    - Use Case: HubSpot is ideal for businesses that integrate their marketing efforts with sales and customer service to create a seamless customer experience. It is particularly useful for nurturing leads through customized workflows and content tailored to each segment.

2. Salesforce Marketing Cloud:

    - Features: This platform offers advanced analytics, marketing automation, and data management capabilities. It enables detailed segmentation based on customer behavior, preferences, and engagement, integrating these insights with campaign management.

- Use Case: Best suited for large organizations that require complex, scalable customer segmentation solutions. Salesforce excels in providing personalized experiences across multiple channels, making it a top choice for enterprises with diverse customer bases.

3. Adobe Experience Cloud:

- Features: Adobe's suite includes analytics, targeting, and campaign management tools that optimize customer experiences. It uses AI and machine learning to help refine customer profiles and segment audiences based on real-time data.

- Use Case: Adobe Experience Cloud is particularly effective for businesses focused on delivering highly personalized content and campaigns. It's an excellent option for companies and retailers combining rich media content with targeted marketing strategies.

These platforms help segment customers and enable businesses to engage each segment with highly personalized marketing campaigns, enhancing both customer satisfaction and business outcomes.

ROI Optimization

Now, let's talk numbers. Optimizing return on investment (ROI) is a cornerstone of any successful marketing strategy. AI provides powerful tools to boost your marketing ROI. By employing predictive modeling, AI can forecast the outcomes of different marketing strategies, allowing you to allocate budgets more effectively. Imagine being able to predict the performance of a campaign before it even launches. AI models can simulate various scenarios based on past campaign data and current market conditions to provide forecasts on campaign reach, customer engagement, and potential sales. This predictive capability enables you to funnel your resources into campaigns and channels that offer the highest return, minimizing waste and maximizing impact.

The magic happens when AI combines these forecasts with real time data, adjusting your marketing strategies dynamically to optimize performance as the campaign unfolds. Suppose an AI system detects a particular campaign is not performing as expected. In that case, it can suggest real-time adjustments such as tweaking your ad copy, modifying the target audience, or even reallocating the budget to more successful channels. This proactive approach to ROI optimization ensures that your marketing efforts are planned with precision and adaptable to ever-changing market dynamics.

In many businesses, AI is becoming a fundamental element that can drive significant improvements in engagement, efficiency, and economic returns.

6.5 LEVERAGING AI FOR COMPETITIVE ANALYSIS

In today's lightning-fast business environment, staying ahead isn't just about keeping pace; it's about predicting the next turn in the road before it even comes into view. This is where AI steps in as a crucial ally in competitive analysis. Imagine having a vigilant system that continuously scans and analyzes your competitors' moves around the clock. This isn't about espionage, but smart, ethical intelligence gathering that can give you a strategic edge. AI systems are particularly adept at monitoring a wide array of digital footprints left by your competitors, from social media activity and online customer reviews to updates on their official websites.

Setting up AI for automated monitoring involves deploying software that tracks specified digital channels and keywords associated with your competitors. This could be anything from new product launches, changes in pricing, or shifts in marketing strategy. AI tools utilize natural language processing to sift through vast amounts of data from these channels, identifying relevant information that could signal a change in your competitors' strategies or reveal new opportunities for your business. For example, suppose a competitor starts focusing heavily on a particular market segment or launches a targeted ad campaign. In that case, AI can quickly bring this to your attention, allowing you to respond or adapt your strategy accordingly.

Going deeper, analyzing your competitors' strategies with AI doesn't just keep you informed; it provides a foundation for strategic decision-making. AI can help dissect the success of competitors' marketing campaigns, giving you insights into what worked and what didn't. It can analyze engagement rates, customer sentiments, and even the reach of digital campaigns, providing a comprehensive view of your competitors' tactics. This analysis helps you understand the 'what' and the 'why' behind competitors' successes. It enables you to fine-tune your strategies. Moreover, AI can simulate potential outcomes based on different strategic scenarios, offering you a range of possible responses and their likely impacts on your market position.

This continuous flow of insights is invaluable for maintaining a competitive edge. AI's ability to provide real-time data and predictive insights allows businesses to stay agile, adapting quickly to new challenges and opportunities. For instance, if AI analysis shows that a competitor's new product is gaining traction quickly, you can immediately strategize how to counteract this move through promotional offers, enhanced product features, or targeted marketing campaigns. This proactive approach ensures you're not just reacting to market changes but consistently staying one step ahead.

In wrapping up our examination of AI-enhanced business strategies, it's clear that AI is not just a tool but a transformative force across various facets of business operations. From refining your business plans with precise data-driven strategies to enhancing customer engagement through chatbots, from predicting market trends to optimizing your marketing efforts and conducting thorough competitive analyses, AI empowers businesses to compete and lead in their industries. However, you'll want to investigate which platform fits your current and future needs. The lists I've provided are a good starting point. If you have a particular need, you can always ask ChatGPT which platform is best for you.

CHAPTER 7:
PERSONAL DEVELOPMENT WITH AI

Let's talk about something that often feels like a roller coaster—managing our health and fitness. If you've ever found yourself stuck in the cycle of dieting and workout fads, you know how overwhelming and frustrating it can be to understand what works for you. But what if I told you that the future of personal health management is already here, and it's tailored precisely to your unique lifestyle and body? Yes, AI is stepping into the fitness and wellness arena as a cheerleader, coach, and game-changer, ready to revolutionize how you approach weight loss and health management.

7.1 A Modern Approach to Personal Health: Losing Weight with AI

Personalized Diet Plans: How AI Can Tailor Diet Plans to Individual Health Metrics and Lifestyle Preferences

Imagine having a nutritionist who intimately knows your dietary preferences, health goals, and lifestyle habits—someone who's available 24/7 and constantly adapts your diet plan based on your progress and feedback. That's what AI does in diet planning. By integrating data from your health trackers, food logs, and even genetic information, AI creates a diet plan that's as unique as your fingerprint. This isn't about generic calorie counting; it's about understanding how different foods interact with your body. For instance, if you're someone who metabolizes carbohydrates quickly but has a dairy sensitivity, AI can customize your meal plans to maximize energy levels while eliminating discomfort and steering you toward your weight loss goals.

The beauty of AI-driven diet plans lies in their adaptability. As you progress, AI learns how your body responds to different dietary adjustments. Did that low-carb week lead to better energy and weight loss? AI takes note and tweaks your plan to include more similar options. It's like having a diet plan that evolves with you, ensuring you stay on track toward your goals without the monotony or frustration of a one-size-fits-all diet.

Here are three notable platforms that leverage AI for diet planning and weight loss:

1. Noom:

  - Features: Noom uses cognitive behavioral therapy (CBT) techniques and AI to personalize weight loss plans for its users. It focuses on making sustainable lifestyle changes rather than quick fixes. The platform offers daily lessons, meal tracking, and personal coaching.

  - Best Use Case: Noom is ideal for individuals looking for a holistic approach to weight loss that includes psychological insights, accountability, and personalized guidance.

2. Lifesum:

  - Features: Lifesum incorporates AI to provide tailored meal plans and recipes based on users' dietary preferences (such as keto, vegetarian, or sugar-free diets) and health goals. It includes features like food tracking, calorie counting, and nutritional advice.

- Best Use Case: Lifesum is best for those who prefer a more self-guided approach emphasizing nutrition and meal planning. It benefits users who want to align their eating habits with specific dietary regimes.

3. Lark Health:

- Features: Lark uses AI-driven chatbots to provide 24/7 personalized coaching and support in diet, weight loss, and chronic disease management, like diabetes. It analyzes user input to give real-time feedback and suggestions.

- Best Use Case: Lark is excellent for individuals who need continuous support and motivation. It's especially beneficial for people managing chronic conditions alongside weight loss, offering an integrated approach to health monitoring.

These platforms leverage AI to provide custom, adaptive guidance, making it easier for individuals to manage their diet and weight loss efforts more effectively.

Activity and Workout Recommendations: Using AI to Suggest Workout Plans Based on Personal Goals, Abilities, and Progress

Now, let's implement those tailored diet plans with personalized workout recommendations. AI doesn't randomly assign exercises; it considers your fitness level, personal preferences, and even the equipment you can access. Whether you enjoy high-intensity interval training or peaceful yoga sessions or are just starting and need something low-impact, AI crafts workout routines that fit into your life seamlessly. Plus, it schedules your workouts based on when you're most energetic or likely to have free time, which means you're more likely to stick to them.

What's truly innovative is how AI adjusts recommendations based on your progress. If you're breezing through your sessions, AI might increase the intensity to keep challenging you. Or, if you're finding it tough to keep up, it can dial back the difficulty to keep things manageable and enjoyable. This dynamic adjustment helps maintain the delicate balance between challenge and motivation, critical factors in making consistent progress.

Here are three platforms that utilize AI technology to enhance fitness planning:

1. Freeletics:

    - Features: Freeletics uses AI to provide personalized workout plans that adjust over time based on user progress and feedback. It offers a wide range of exercises that can be done with minimal or no equipment, focusing on bodyweight routines.

    - Best Use Case: Ideal for individuals seeking flexibility and a personalized fitness routine that can be performed anywhere, anytime, without gym equipment.

2. Fitbit:

    - Features: Fitbit uses AI to create tailored workout plans based on available equipment, individual strength, fitness levels, and recovery state. It suggests exercises to ensure balanced muscle use and optimal gains.

    - Best Use Case: Fitbit is excellent for gym-goers who want a customized, effective training plan that adapts to the equipment they have available, whether at home or in a gym.

3. Vi Trainer:

- Features: Vi Trainer offers a unique AI-powered digital personal trainer that delivers audio coaching. The AI learns and adapts to your fitness needs and goals, providing real-time feedback during workouts.

- Best Use Case: Vi Trainer is best for runners and cyclists who prefer guided training sessions. It is particularly useful for those who enjoy outdoor activities or treadmill workouts and seek motivational, adaptive coaching through headphones.

These platforms leverage AI to ensure that your fitness journey is guided by intelligent, adaptive technology, making your workouts more effective and personalized. Whether working out at home, in a gym, or outdoors, these tools can help you optimize your exercise regimen.

Monitoring and Adjustments: The Role of AI in Monitoring Progress and Adjusting Lifestyle Plans for Optimal Results

Monitoring progress is one of the most critical aspects of any weight loss journey. But rather than just stepping on a scale, AI gives you a comprehensive view of how you're doing. These programs can provide analytics about everything from your sleep patterns and calorie intake to your heart rate variability and workout performance by analyzing data from fitness trackers and health apps. This holistic approach allows precise adjustments to your diet and exercise plans, ensuring you're always moving towards your goals effectively.

But it's not just about numbers and data; it's about understanding your body's signals. For instance, if AI notices that your stress levels are consistently high, it might suggest incorporating more mindfulness and recovery activities into your routine to prevent burnout. This proactive adjustment ability ensures that your journey toward health is balanced and sustainable.

As we continue to explore the capabilities of AI in personal health management, it's clear that this technology is not just about making incremental changes; it's about transforming lives. It offers a personalized approach that respects our uniqueness and adapts to our evolving needs. It makes health and fitness journeys less about struggle and more about personal growth and discovery. As you consider integrating AI into your health regimen, remember that this technology is here to support you every step of the way, making your path to wellness attainable and enjoyable.

7.2 LIFESTYLE: PUTTING AI TO WORK FOR YOUR HEALTH

Integrating with Wearables: How AI Works with Wearable Technology to Tailor Workouts in Real Time Based on Physiological Data

Let's lace up those sneakers and discuss how AI transforms your workout routines through seamless integration with wearable technology. Your fitness tracker does more than count steps or monitor your heart rate—it feeds valuable data to AI systems that craft and adjust your workout plans in real time. The Fitbit and the Apple Watch are the most common, but several others have compelling uses. I personally like the Aura Ring and Garmin Watch. This integration allows for a highly personalized fitness regimen that responds to your body's immediate needs. For instance, if your wearable detects an elevated heart rate or increased fatigue, AI can adjust the intensity of your scheduled workout, suggesting lighter activities or even recommending a rest day if needed.

This intelligent collaboration continues beyond there. AI can analyze long-term data from your wearables to track your progress and adapt your workout plans to challenge you as your fitness level improves continuously. It also considers recovery times, helping you balance striving for peak performance and avoiding overtraining. This thoughtful, informed approach ensures that your workouts are effective and safe, keeping your overall well-being at the forefront.

Engagement and Motivation: Using AI to Keep Individuals Engaged and Motivated Through Personalized Feedback and Encouragement

Staying motivated can often be the most challenging part of maintaining a health and fitness regimen. Here's where AI shines, acting as your cheerleader and coach rolled into one. Through regular, personalized feedback, AI technology can help you recognize your achievements, no matter how small, and encourage you to keep pushing forward. It can send you celebratory messages when you hit a new personal best or gentle reminders if you start falling off track. This constant, supportive communication is tailored to your personality and motivational style, whether you need gentle nudges or enthusiastic encouragement.

Moreover, AI can gamify your health journey by setting up challenges and rewards that make sticking to your meal plans and workout schedules exciting. Imagine competing in a virtual race or achieving monthly health goals in exchange for rewards like new recipes or workout gear. This fun element keeps the routine fresh and engaging, making your health journey enjoyable rather than something you feel obligated to stick to.

Tracking Progress: The Importance of AI in Tracking and Visualizing Progress Toward Meal and Fitness Goals

Visualizing your progress is incredibly satisfying and can be an essential part of staying motivated. AI excels in this area by compiling data from your meals, workouts, and health metrics to create comprehensive progress reports. These aren't just dry spreadsheets; they're visually engaging charts and graphs that show you how far you've come and how close you are to your goals. For instance, you might see a graph illustrating how your dietary fiber intake has improved over the months or a chart showing the gradual increase in your strength training weights.

These visual tools track where you've been and help plan where you're going, adjusting your future meal and workout plans to ensure you continue to progress. Seeing the tangible results of your efforts can be incredibly rewarding, reinforcing your commitment to your health goals and inspiring you to keep pushing forward. Whether you're looking to shed a few pounds, build strength, or just feel healthier, AI's role in tracking and visualizing your journey is a crucial component that transforms your aspirations into achievable, measurable successes.

7.3 INTELLECTUAL DEVELOPMENT: LEARNING A NEW LANGUAGE WITH AI ASSISTANCE

Imagine picking up a new language, not through the old-school method of flipping through dusty textbooks, but through an interactive, engaging AI system that adapts to your learning style and pace. That's the reality AI brings to language learning today. It crafts a learning journey so personal and intuitive that it feels like the program knows everything you need before even you do. Whether you're gearing up for a vacation in Italy, aiming to expand your business in China, or just exploring a personal passion, AI language learning tools are like having an always-available, infinitely patient, and highly adaptive tutor.

Personalized Learning Paths: How AI Creates Personalized Language Learning Experiences Based on Learner Pace and Style

The magic of AI in language learning lies in its ability to create highly personalized learning paths. AI can tailor your coursework to better suit your needs by analyzing your initial language skills and learning preferences. For instance, if you're a visual learner, it might focus on delivering content through videos and interactive graphics.

Conversely, learning better through practice might increase the frequency of interactive quizzes and conversational practice exercises. AI also adapts to your pace, offering extra help and practice in areas where you're struggling and speeding up through the parts you master quickly.

This personalized approach extends to scheduling. Knowing that consistency is vital in language learning, AI tools can gently nudge you to study when you've historically been most receptive, maybe early in the morning with a fresh cup of coffee or during the lunch break when you need a mental shift. It learns from your daily routines and adapts, making learning effective and a seamlessly integrated part of your day.

Interactive Tools and Resources: Highlighting AI-Powered Tools and Resources That Make Language Learning More Interactive and Effective

One of the standout features of AI in language learning is the range of interactive tools and resources it brings to your fingertips. These tools transform learning from a passive to an active process. Voice recognition technology, for example, allows you to practice pronunciation until you get it just right. This tech isn't just about right or wrong; it provides feedback on how to move your tongue or shape your lips to mimic native pronunciation closely.

For the next phase of language learning, there are AI-powered chatbots, designed to converse with you in your new language. These bots provide the practice needed to build confidence and the scaffolding to ensure you're continually learning from the interaction. They can role-play different scenarios, from ordering food in a restaurant to negotiating a contract, providing a safe space for you to test your language skills without the fear of embarrassment.

Overcoming Language Barriers: How AI Can Help Overcome Common Language Learning Barriers

AI technology is particularly adept at breaking down two of the biggest hurdles in language learning: pronunciation and grammar. Through sophisticated speech recognition, AI tools listen to your pronunciation and offer immediate correction and feedback, much like a personal language coach would. This instant feedback loop accelerates the learning process and builds correct habits immediately.

Grammar, often the bane of language learners, is another area where AI excels. By analyzing hundreds of thousands of text and speech examples, AI can teach grammar in context, which is far more effective than memorizing rules. It presents you with patterns that native speakers use, integrates them into interactive exercises, and corrects your sentences. This helps learners understand not just the 'how' but also the 'why' behind grammatical structures.

Here are two notable platforms that leverage AI to personalize language learning using voice and written methods:

1. Duolingo:

    - Features: Duolingo uses AI-driven algorithms to adapt lessons to the user's learning style and pace. It provides interactive lessons in reading, writing, speaking, and listening. The app personalizes the difficulty of exercises based on user performance. It offers immediate feedback on pronunciation and grammar through its speech recognition technology.

    - Best Use Case: Duolingo is excellent for learners of all levels who want a comprehensive, game-like approach to language learning. It's particularly useful for beginners and intermediate learners looking to develop basic fluency and conversational skills in a new language.

2. Rosetta Stone:

- Features: Rosetta Stone uses a speech-recognition engine to improve pronunciation and speaking skills. It compares the learner's voice to native speakers and provides corrective feedback. It also customizes the learning path by analyzing user responses and adapting the curriculum to focus on areas of difficulty.

- Best Use Case: Rosetta Stone is ideal for learners who want a more immersive experience and focus heavily on speaking and listening skills. It is well-suited for users who prefer learning through context and visual cues and aim for proficiency in everyday conversational skills.

These platforms not only offer extensive language learning tools but also incorporate AI to create a personalized and adaptive learning environment, enhancing the efficiency and enjoyment of mastering a new language.

As you embark on your own language-learning adventure, remember that AI is here to guide you through every step, making the process educational and enjoyable.

7.4 PERSONAL DEVELOPMENT: SETTING AND ACHIEVING GOALS WITH AI

Goal Setting with AI: Utilizing AI to Help Set Realistic, Achievable Goals Based on Personal Data and Trends

When it comes to setting goals, whether they're related to fitness, learning, or personal development, the challenge isn't just in defining what you want to achieve but also in figuring out the realistic steps to get there. This is where AI steps in, transforming the art of goal setting into a science that's tailored just for you. By analyzing patterns in your behavior, preferences, and past achievements, AI can help you set goals that are not just aspirational but also attainable. Picture this: you want to run a marathon but never run more than a mile. An AI system can help break down this lofty goal into smaller, manageable milestones, such as increasing your longest run by 10% each week. It uses data—like your current fitness level and progress over time—to adjust these milestones, ensuring they always align with your capabilities and schedule.

What makes AI incredibly effective in this domain is its ability to sift through and make sense of vast amounts of personal development data. From your daily step count and sleep patterns to your eating habits and leisure activities, AI gathers insights that inform your goal-setting process. This isn't about pushing you towards generic targets but crafting personalized objectives that fit seamlessly into your life and continuously adapt as your circumstances and priorities evolve. Moreover, by setting dynamically adjustable goals, AI ensures that your targets remain challenging yet achievable, keeping motivation and frustration low. This customized approach enhances your likelihood of success. It makes the journey towards your goals more enjoyable and aligned with your personal growth.

Monitoring and Guidance: How AI Can Provide Keep Individuals on Track Towards Their Goals

Now, setting goals is just the beginning. The real magic of AI comes into play in its role as a constant guide and monitor. Think of AI as a dedicated coach who never misses a beat, always there to offer insights and encouragement. AI can provide real-time feedback and actionable advice by continuously tracking your activities and progress. For instance, if your goal is to improve sleep quality, AI can analyze data from your sleep tracker, identify patterns that may be disrupting your sleep, and suggest practical interventions like adjusting your bedtime or reducing evening screen time.

This ongoing monitoring extends beyond mere data tracking; it involves understanding the context of your progress—or lack thereof. If you're falling short of your weekly goals, AI isn't there to nudge you; it's there to understand why. Was it a particularly stressful week at work, or were there other disruptions in your routine? By considering these factors, AI can offer tailored advice that addresses the root cause of setbacks rather than just the symptoms. This kind of nuanced guidance helps you stay on track realistically, adjusting your path forward based on actual life events, significantly increasing your resilience and capacity to achieve long-term goals.

Adjusting Strategies: The Role of AI in Strategy Adjustment Based on Progress and Changing Circumstances

Adaptability is key in any long-term plan. AI excels in this area by dynamically adjusting your strategies based on ongoing feedback and changing circumstances. Your initial plan was to dedicate an hour daily to learning that new language. However, AI might notice that your performance and engagement drop after 30 minutes. This insight suggests splitting your learning into two 30-minute sessions, potentially increasing retention and reducing burnout.

Moreover, AI's ability to integrate various data sources provides a holistic view of your lifestyle, enabling it to make interconnected suggestions. For example, suppose you're training for a physical event and trying to cut down on sugar. In that case, AI can correlate your dietary habits with your workout effectiveness and suggest nutritional adjustments to support your physical goals. This interconnected approach ensures that the adjustments AI proposes are comprehensive and consider the big picture of your well-being rather than isolated aspects of your lifestyle.

Visualization of Success: Using AI to Visualize Potential Outcomes and Success Paths, Enhancing Motivation

Finally, one of the most compelling features of AI in goal setting and achievement is its ability to project and visualize potential outcomes. This isn't just about predicting success; it's about showing you what it could look like. Through data visualization, AI can create detailed projections and what-if scenarios that help you see the possible futures based on different choices and efforts. For instance, if you're saving for a trip or a big purchase, AI can show you how adjusting your monthly savings by even a tiny amount could shorten your time to reach your goal.

These visual projections are incredibly motivating, turning abstract goals into tangible outcomes you can see and practically aim for. Plus, by providing a clear visual roadmap of your progress and future path, AI helps reinforce your commitment to your goals, keeping you engaged and invested in the process. This visualization is a reminder of what you're working towards and a beacon of hope and motivation, especially when the going gets tough.

Here are two platforms explicitly designed for broader life goals:

1. Strides:

    - Features: Strides is an app that uses AI to help users track and achieve goals through habit tracking and intelligent reminders. It allows for setting up and monitoring various goals, such as personal development, financial, educational, and more. The app uses data to provide personalized insights and predictions on user progress.

    - Best Use Case: Strides is ideal for individuals who need a comprehensive tool to track a wide range of personal and professional goals. It is particularly useful for those who appreciate a visually engaging and intuitive interface for monitoring their habits and achievements.

2. GoalsOnTrack:

    - Features: GoalsOnTrack incorporates AI to help users structure their goals using the SMART criteria (Specific, Measurable, Attainable, Relevant, Time-bound) and visualizes progress with detailed charts and reports. It supports habit tracking, journaling, and personalized goal templates.

    - Best Use Case: GoalsOnTrack is suitable for users looking for a structured approach to goal setting, especially for complex or long-term objectives. It is great for professionals and students who benefit from visual goal planning and detailed progress monitoring.

These platforms leverage AI to not only help you set and manage your goals but also to provide intelligent feedback and encouragement, making the process of achieving your life goals more structured and supported.

7.5 PERSONAL FINANCE DEVELOPMENT: MANAGING PERSONAL FINANCES WITH AI

Navigating the world of personal finance can sometimes feel like trying to solve a complex puzzle with pieces that don't fit. But what if you had a tool that helped you find the right pieces and showed you how they fit together to create a clear financial picture? That's exactly what AI is doing in personal finance management. It's like having a financial advisor in your pocket, powered by algorithms and big data, ready to offer insights and guidance tailored just for you.

Automated Financial Planning: Introducing AI Tools That Can Automate the Creation of Personal Financial Plans and Budgets

Imagine a world where your budget practically manages itself. AI tools in financial planning are turning this into a reality by automating the mundane yet crucial tasks of budgeting and financial planning. These tools work by first understanding your income, expenses, and financial goals. From there, they create a personalized budget that tracks your spending and automatically adjusts to your financial habits. For instance, if you tend to overspend on dining out, AI can tweak your monthly budget allocations, suggesting areas where you can cut back to keep your finances balanced.

But it's not just about tracking and adjusting. AI financial tools can also predict future spending patterns based on past behavior, giving you a heads-up on potential budget shortfalls. This proactive approach allows you to adjust before issues arise, ensuring you're always on track to meet your financial goals. Plus, these tools can integrate with your bank accounts and financial services, providing a seamless financial management experience that keeps all your financial data in one place, updated in real time.

Investment Advice: How AI Can Provide Personalized Investment Advice Based on Risk Tolerance and Financial Goals

When it comes to investments, one size does not fit all. That's where AI comes in, offering personalized investment advice tailored to your unique financial situation and risk tolerance. By analyzing vast amounts of market data and trends, AI can identify investment opportunities that match your risk profile and financial goals. Whether you're a conservative investor looking for stable returns or a more aggressive investor aiming for high growth, AI can provide recommendations that suit your style.

AI-driven investment tools continuously monitor the market, adjusting your investment strategy based on changing conditions and new data. This dynamic approach ensures that your portfolio always aligns with the best opportunities available, maximizing your potential returns while managing risk. And because these tools learn from each interaction, they better predict which investments are most likely to meet your expectations over time, making your investment journey smoother and more predictable.

Expense Tracking and Analysis: Leveraging AI to Track and Analyze Expenses, Identifying Opportunities to Save

Keeping track of where your money goes is one of the first steps in controlling your finances. AI excels in this area by automatically categorizing your expenses and providing a detailed analysis of your spending patterns. This isn't just about knowing how much you spent last month on groceries or utilities; it's about understanding your spending habits and identifying areas where you can save.

AI tools analyze your transactions, highlighting trends such as seasonal spending spikes or recurring subscriptions you might not need. They can alert you to unusual activity, such as a duplicate charge or a sudden increase in a regular payment, helping you avoid overpaying. By providing these insights, AI enables you to keep a tighter rein on your expenses and empowers you to make informed decisions about your money, saving you significantly over time.

Financial Health Monitoring: The Importance of AI in Providing a Holistic View of Financial Health and Making Recommendations for Improvement

Finally, AI's role in monitoring your overall financial health cannot be overstated. By considering not just your spending and savings but also your debts, investments, and financial goals, AI provides a 360-degree view of your financial situation. This comprehensive analysis allows you to see how all aspects of your finances are interconnected and how changes in one area can affect others.

AI tools can also recommend ways to improve your financial health, such as adjusting your savings rate, refinancing debts, or changing your investment allocations. These recommendations are based on simulations that consider various scenarios and their potential impacts on your finances, giving you a clear roadmap for achieving financial stability and growth.

As we wrap up this exploration of AI in personal finance, it's clear that AI is not just changing the way we manage our money—it's revolutionizing it. From automating budgets and providing personalized investment advice to tracking expenses and monitoring financial health, AI empowers you to take control of your finances with confidence and precision. As you leverage these AI tools, remember that they are not just about keeping your finances in order; they're about helping you achieve your financial dreams, one smart decision at a time.

Here are three powerful tools that cater to various aspects of personal finance management:

1. Mint:

    - Features: Mint uses AI to categorize transactions automatically, track spending patterns, and create budgets based on user behavior. It also provides alerts on unusual charges and offers personalized insights into saving more money. The platform aggregates all your financial accounts, including bank accounts, credit cards, loans, and investments.

    - Use Case: Mint is ideal for individuals looking to view their finances and improve budgeting habits comprehensively. It's particularly effective for those who need help organizing their finances and want alerts on bills and low balances.

2. Personal Capital:

    - Features: This app combines AI with professional financial advisory services. It provides budgeting and retirement planning tools, and its strength lies in investment management. Personal Capital uses AI to analyze investment portfolios to assess risk, track performance, and suggest optimizations based on the user's financial goals.

- Use Case: Personal Capital is best for individuals with a significant investment portfolio who want detailed insights and financial planning advice. It's precious for those nearing retirement or needing advanced wealth management services.

3. Betterment:

- Features: Betterment uses AI to manage investments through robo-advisory services. It offers automated portfolio management tailored to user goals, tax-loss harvesting, and rebalancing. The platform also provides retirement planning tools and customized financial advice.

- Use Case: Betterment is excellent for those looking for a hands-off investment strategy that still offers personalized, AI-driven advice. It's suited for beginners to invest as well as those looking for detailed tax optimization and retirement planning.

These platforms leverage AI technology to provide tailored financial insights, automate tasks, and help users make informed financial decisions, from day-to-day budgeting to long-term investment strategies.

CHAPTER 8:
BEYOND THE BASICS WITH GENERATIVE AI TOOLS

Picture this: you're standing in front of a canvas; your palette is not just made up of colors but a blend of data, algorithms, and a splash of creativity, all ready to be transformed into a masterpiece. That's the evolving world of AI art generation for you. It's not just about letting a computer take the wheel; it's about merging the best of two worlds—traditional artistic techniques and cutting-edge AI technologies—to push the boundaries of what's creatively possible. Whether you're an artist intrigued by the digital wave or a technophile with a soft spot for the arts, the fusion of AI and art is a playground of possibilities just waiting for you to step in and explore.

8.1 ADVANCED TECHNIQUES IN AI ART GENERATION

Pushing the Boundaries: Exploring cutting-edge techniques in AI art generation that go beyond basic applications, pushing the boundaries of creativity.

Let's dive deeper into the heart of AI art generation, where fascinating new art techniques are breaking ground. Imagine AI not just as a tool that replicates styles or generates what's been fed into it but as a partner in creativity. Advanced techniques now allow AI to interpret emotional cues from music, literature, or even social media trends, translating these into visual representations that are both abstract and deeply meaningful. For instance, an AI analyzing the tone and mood of a set of poems could generate artwork that visually represents the emotional spectrum of the literature—capturing the essence of melancholy or joy in colors and shapes. This depth goes beyond traditional art generation, offering a new layer of interaction between AI and human emotion, pushing the creative dialogue to new heights.

You can use DALL-E and RunwayML as platforms for advanced art creation, but you add breakthrough technologies like Artbreeder to your tool kit. It allows users to manipulate genres of images to change styles and features, offering a collaborative and highly customizable approach to art generation. Users can merge different artworks or photographic styles to produce novel visual outputs.

Interactivity and AI

Now, think about art that doesn't just sit on a wall. Interactive AI art is about creating pieces that respond to and evolve with the audience. This could be through motion sensors that change the artwork based on the viewer's movements or AI that adapts the piece based on real-time social media inputs. For example, an AI-driven installation at a music festival might change colors and patterns in response to the collective mood of the crowd, measured through the volume of the music or the social media posts coming out of the event. This kind of interactivity transforms viewers into participants, creating a dynamic art experience that is perpetually unique and engaging.

Here are two platforms that can generate interactive art and forms:

1. DeepDream

    • Initially developed by Google, DeepDream is an AI program that uses a convolutional neural network to find and enhance image patterns via algorithmic pareidolia. It is particularly known for creating surreal and psychedelic visuals that users can interactively alter. This interaction can involve changing layers, filters, or the content of the images to see how DeepDream interprets and transforms them.

- *Advanced Prompt:* "Create a DeepDream visualization that explores the concept of 'oceanic dreams.' Begin with a base image of an underwater coral reef and progressively enhance it with dream-like features reminiscent of sea creatures mixed with celestial objects. Allow users to adjust parameters such as the intensity of the dream features, the types of creatures blended (marine vs. celestial), and the color palette, creating a dynamic, evolving dream sequence."

- 2. TouchDesigner

  - TouchDesigner is a node-based visual programming language platform for real-time interactive multimedia content. It is suitable for both artists and programmers to create interactive installations, performances, and multimedia experiences. The AI aspect is incorporated through its ability to interface with machine learning models, allowing users to integrate AI-generated content in real-time environments.

  - *Advanced Prompt:* "Design an interactive installation using TouchDesigner that responds to the audience's movements and sounds. The installation should project a forest made of dynamic, fractal trees that grow and change colors based on the audience's proximity and the volume of their voices. Include elements such as falling leaves or animals that appear when certain conditions are met and allow the audience to control weather effects in the virtual forest, such as rain or fog, by their gestures and noises."

Hybrid Artistic Approaches: Detailed exploration of combining traditional art techniques with AI-generated elements to create unique hybrid artwork

Novel ways of creating original art pieces can start with blending the old with the new; hybrid artistic approaches merge traditional art forms with AI-generated elements to create something unique. Think of a painter who uses AI to create complex geometric backgrounds on which they hand-paint portraits or sculptors who design their pieces with AI before crafting them from physical materials. This approach enhances artistic possibilities and retains the human touch that many fear will be lost in the digital age. Using AI as a tool in their creative arsenal, artists can explore new realms of creativity, pushing their traditional methodologies into the modern era without losing the essence of their personal artistic touch.

As you continue exploring AI's fascinating capabilities in art, remember that this isn't about replacing the artist. It's about expanding what you, the artist, can do, creating new avenues for expression and experimentation. Whether you're a creator, a curator, a technologist, or simply an art enthusiast, the evolving tools of AI art generation offer a canvas where the only limit is your imagination.

8.2 CREATING COMPLEX MUSIC COMPOSITIONS WITH AI

This is the world of advanced AI music composition, where technology and creativity merge to push musical boundaries far beyond traditional methods.

When discussing advanced concepts in AI music composition, we're referring to more than just generating tunes. AI can now understand and apply music theory, algorithmic composition techniques, and even the emotional context of music. For instance, algorithmic composition involves creating music based on a set of rules or algorithms without direct human input. AI systems can be programmed with these rules and given the autonomy to develop, resulting in compositions that might be impossible for human composers to conceive. Moreover, AI can analyze extensive music databases to identify patterns and styles and then apply these to create innovative compositions that maintain a stylistic integrity that's both familiar and refreshingly new.

Another exciting development is the integration of AI in live performances. Imagine attending a concert where an AI partially composed the music in real time. This AI analyzes the audience's reactions—perhaps through sound levels, facial expressions, or social media feedback—and adjusts the music accordingly, enhancing the engagement and experience of the concertgoers. This real-time compositional adjustment represents a groundbreaking shift in live performances, blending human performance art with machine intelligence to create a dynamic, interactive musical experience.

The ability of AI to add emotional depth and complexity to music is particularly noteworthy. Traditionally, conveying emotion through music has been the domain of human composers who draw on personal experiences and cultural contexts. AI, however, can now be trained to recognize emotional cues in music and use this understanding to compose pieces that evoke specific feelings. By analyzing the key, tempo, rhythm, and harmonic progressions associated with different emotions in music, AI can generate compositions that move listeners in intended emotional directions, from joy and excitement to melancholy and calm. This capability makes AI an invaluable tool for film scorers or any project where music is used to enhance emotional storytelling.

Exploring collaborative projects between human musicians and AI, we see a symbiosis that enhances both the creative process and the resulting musical works. Musicians can input thematic ideas, emotional tones, or even rough melodies into an AI system, which then processes this input to produce refined musical pieces or suggest variations that might not have been initially considered. This collaboration amplifies human creativity through AI's computational power, leading to innovative musical creations that might not have been possible otherwise. For example, a project might involve an AI that takes a simple melody composed by a human and develops it into a full orchestral score, suggesting harmonizations and counterpoints that enrich the original piece.

Several innovative tools and platforms facilitate complex music compositions. We've discussed AIVA (Artificial Intelligence Virtual Artist), and there's another popular platform, Amper Music. They are both at the forefront, offering tools that allow users, from professional musicians to hobbyists, to create music using AI. These platforms provide user-friendly interfaces where users can input styles, moods, and other parameters, and the AI generates music based on the inputs. The outcomes are both musically pleasing and highly original, providing users with a rich palette of sounds and styles that can be further customized or used as is for various projects, from video game soundtracks to YouTube videos and beyond.

Here's an example of an advanced prompt for each platform:

1. AIVA (Artificial Intelligence Virtual Artist)

    *   ***Advanced Prompt:*** "Compose a symphonic piece that depicts the journey of a comet through space. Start with a slow, mysterious introduction using low strings and woodwinds to represent the vastness of space. Gradually introduce a theme with brass and choirs to signify the comet's discovery. Build momentum with faster tempos and higher pitches as the comet approaches the sun, incorporating orchestral crescendos to represent the intensifying solar winds. Conclude with a majestic forte using the full orchestra

as the comet passes the sun and continues its journey into the unknown."

2. Amper Music

- ***Advanced Prompt:*** "Create an evolving electronic track that mimics the lifecycle of a futuristic city. Begin with minimalistic, digital sounds to represent the city's foundation. As the city develops, layer in complex rhythms and a mix of synthesized and traditional instruments to symbolize technological advancements and bustling life. Include dynamic changes in tempo and volume to reflect the city's day and night cycles. Introduce dissonant chords to represent challenges the city faces, and resolve with harmonious sections as solutions are found. Allow the piece to gradually return to minimalism, depicting the city's eventual serene decline into obsolescence."

Whether you are a seasoned musician or an enthusiast intrigued by the confluence of tech and music, the AI tools available today offer a new realm of musical exploration and expression that is exciting, accessible, and endlessly creative.

8.3 DEVELOPING AI-GENERATED VIDEO CONTENT FOR SOCIAL MEDIA

Let's talk about making videos that catch the eye and capture your audience's imagination on social media. It's about creating content that lives and breathes the trends, making your mark with every upload. AI-generated video content is rapidly becoming a game-changer in this arena. It's not just about cutting down on the grunt work; it's about leveraging AI to tap into the pulse of social media trends, creating content that resonates, engages, and spreads like wildfire. Today, AI tools are equipped to analyze social media data in real time, identifying emerging trends early–from the latest dance challenges to viral marketing campaigns. These tools can then generate video content that aligns with trends, ensuring that what you produce is always on point.

Imagine AI systems that track and analyze the performance of various content formats across different platforms and times, identifying what type of content works best and when. This isn't just about following trends; it's about predicting them. For instance, if an AI tool notices a rising interest in a particular type of challenge video or a style of visual humor, it can prompt you to create content that taps into this burgeoning interest, giving you a first-mover advantage in capturing audience attention. Beyond trend tracking, AI is pushing the boundaries of personalization. It's about creating content that speaks directly to your audience. Using data from viewer preferences and behaviors, AI tools can craft personalized video messages that speak directly to viewers' interests, past interactions, or even their current mood. This level of personalization boosts engagement and fosters a deeper connection between your brand and your audience, making your social media channels a must-visit space.

Now, let's shift gears and talk about the nuts and bolts–video production. Traditionally, video production has been resource-intensive, requiring hours of human effort from scripting and shooting to editing and post-production. AI is revolutionizing this process, making it faster and more cost-effective. You can automate much of the production process with AI-powered video creation tools. These tools can generate raw video clips based on textual descriptions, assemble these clips into coherent narratives, and even add effects and transitions based on your chosen style and tone. This automation drastically cuts production time, allowing you to churn out high-quality content faster. It's a boon, especially for platforms like TikTok or Instagram, where the speed of content creation can be as crucial as the content itself.

Two such platforms include Lumen5 and Magisto, and again, I've provided examples of advanced prompts for each.

1. Lumen5

    - Lumen5 is an AI-driven video creation platform that helps users turn blog posts, articles, and other text content into engaging videos optimized for social media. The platform uses natural language processing to automatically structure storyboards based on the input text and suggests relevant visuals and transitions. Users can customize the video by adjusting layouts, choosing themes, and adding music, making it a popular tool for marketers and content creators who want to quickly produce eye-catching social media content.

    - ***Advanced Prompt:*** "Create a dynamic and visually engaging video from a blog post titled 'The Future of Renewable Energy.' Highlight key points such as the latest advancements in solar technology, wind energy efficiencies, and the economic impacts of adopting renewable sources. Use high-quality images of solar panels, wind turbines, and bustling cityscapes using green technology. Incorporate upbeat and inspiring background music to enhance viewer engagement. Tailor the video's pacing to be fast and include pop-up text to emphasize important statistics and quotes, making it perfect for sharing across social media platforms like LinkedIn and Twitter."

1. Magisto

    - Magisto, powered by AI, automates the video editing process using emotion sense technology to analyze and edit raw video footage and photos. Users select a style, add music, and upload their clips. Magisto's AI editor compiles these into polished videos designed to capture viewers' attention on social media platforms. The platform is particularly adept at creating emotionally engaging videos tailored to the user's desired audience, which is critical for effective social media marketing.

- **Advanced Prompt:** "Produce a captivating short film showcasing a day in the life of a small-town bakery using customer-submitted video clips and photos. The video should convey the warmth and community vibe of the bakery, highlighting moments like the early morning preparation of bread, the welcoming smiles of staff, and the customers' joy as they taste various pastries. Use a nostalgic filter and a light, acoustic music track to enhance the cozy, inviting atmosphere of the bakery. End with customer testimonials about their favorite bakery items, edited to emphasize emotional expressions and reactions, ideal for Facebook and Instagram stories."

From tapping into the latest trends and creating personalized content to streamlining the production process, AI tools empower creators and brands to enhance their digital presence and connect with their audiences more meaningfully and engagingly. So, exploring AI-generated video content might be your next best move, whether you're looking to spice up your social media feed, grow your follower base, or engage your audience in new and innovative ways.

8.4 Daily Tasks Automated Using AI

Imagine waking up to a world where your daily routine is manageable and effortlessly streamlined. That's the promise of AI when it comes to automating your everyday tasks. Whether it's sorting through your overflowing email inbox, scheduling meetings, or even curating content for your next social media post, AI is there to lift the burden off your shoulders. Let's start by identifying which of your daily tasks are prime candidates for AI automation. Think about the repetitive tasks that consume your time without adding value to your day. It could be filtering spam emails, entering data, or managing your calendar. These tasks are perfect for automation because they follow predictable patterns that AI can learn and optimize.

Now, diving into the tools and techniques available for automation, the landscape is rich with options. For email management, AI-powered tools can categorize emails, highlight the most important ones, and suggest short responses. Imagine an AI that learns your priorities and ensures you get all the essential messages amidst the clutter. For scheduling, AI assistants can coordinate between different calendars to find the best meeting times, send invites, and even reschedule appointments as conflicts arise—all without you needing to lift a finger.

But as we integrate AI into our daily routines, it's crucial to maintain a balance between automation and the human touch. While AI can handle most of the workload, human insights, creativity, and personal touch often make the difference. In customer service, for instance, an AI can field initial inquiries. Still, a human agent might be better suited for handling complex issues or providing personal empathy and understanding. This balance ensures that while efficiency is gained, the quality of interaction and service remains high, reflecting your brand's or personal ethos's actual value.

The benefits of automating daily tasks with AI are transformative; however, choosing the right platform to suit your needs is very important. For example, "x.ai" is best used for scheduling meetings, and Boomerang for Gmail is more robust for email sorting and assistance. When using such platforms, the improved work-life balance can't be overstated. With AI shouldering the burden of mundane tasks, you can reclaim time for yourself, whether it's for professional growth, personal hobbies, or spending time with loved ones.

AI is not just a tool for enhancing productivity; it's a partner redefining how you navigate your daily life. By offloading the mundane, you're free to focus on the creative, the strategic, and the meaningful.

CHAPTER 9:
ENGAGING WITH THE AI COMMUNITY

Imagine stepping into a bustling, vibrant city where every corner, every café, and every park is buzzing with innovators, thinkers, and creators all speaking the language of AI. This city isn't on any map but in both the digital world and local meetups where AI enthusiasts like you gather. These communities are goldmines of knowledge, networking opportunities, and the latest AI developments. They're places where questions, big or small, find answers and where ideas can blossom into projects or even startups. If you've ever felt alone on your AI journey, these communities are where you find your tribe.

9.1 JOINING AI COMMUNITIES: WHY AND HOW

Benefits of Community Engagement

Joining an AI community is one of the smartest moves on your AI adventure. First off, communities are incredible repositories of knowledge. Whether you're a beginner or someone with intermediate knowledge, there's always something new to learn, and what better way than from real people who have faced and overcome similar challenges? These communities are pulsing with discussions, webinars, and posts about the latest AI developments—imagine having access to cutting-edge AI news before it even hits the mainstream tech blogs!

Networking is another colossal benefit. These communities connect you with hobbyists, professionals, and experts whose insights and experiences are invaluable. Who knows? The person you talk with about neural networks may be looking for someone with your exact skill set for a new project. As AI continues to evolve, staying informed through these networks can be crucial for your long-term career growth.

Finding the Right Community

So, how do you find the right AI community? Start by considering your interests and career goals. Are you fascinated by machine learning, or does the realm of robotics capture your imagination? You may be interested in how AI can be leveraged in healthcare or finance. Whatever your niche, there's likely a community for it—online platforms like LinkedIn, Reddit, and even Facebook host myriad groups dedicated to specific AI interests. Websites like Meetup can be great for finding local AI clubs or study groups.

When choosing a community, look for one that matches your interests and commitment level. Some groups are highly technical and might be suited for those delving into the intricacies of AI programming. In contrast, others focus more broadly on AI impacts and applications, which can be great for beginners and intermediates alike.

Active Participation

Active participation is key to making the most out of AI communities. Don't just lurk—engage! Start by joining discussions or threads. Ask questions, share your insights, or even post interesting articles you've come across. Many online forums also hold virtual meetups or challenges, which can be a fantastic way to get involved and showcase your skills.

Contributing content can also be incredibly rewarding. If you've worked on a project or developed a unique AI model, share your experiences. Not only will this help others, but it will also establish your reputation within the community. Remember, active participation is a two-way street that benefits you and the community. It enhances your learning and solidifies your standing as an engaged member.

Building a Personal Brand

Engaging in AI communities offers an excellent opportunity to build your brand. As you interact and share your knowledge, you gradually become recognized as a knowledgeable and reliable member. This recognition can be pivotal for your professional growth. Consider creating content that adds value—detailed blog posts, helpful guides, or even tutorial videos.

Showcasing your projects or case studies highlights your expertise and ability to apply AI in practical scenarios. Make sure to highlight how your work can solve problems or push the boundaries of current technology. As you build your brand, you also increase your visibility in AI, opening doors to new opportunities, collaborations, and even career advancements.

In essence, AI communities are about what you can learn from them and how you can contribute and grow. They provide a platform for education, innovation, and professional development. Whether online or in person, these communities offer a space to connect, collaborate, and contribute, helping you navigate AI's ever-evolving landscape with confidence and support.

9.2 CONTRIBUTING TO OPEN-SOURCE AI PROJECTS

Diving into the world of open-source AI projects is like stepping into a vibrant workshop where everyone is busily crafting, refining, and sharing tools that could one day change the world. In the realm of AI, open-source means more than just openly available code. It embodies a spirit of collaboration and innovation. If you've ever felt the urge to contribute to something larger than yourself, to leave a mark on the evolving story of AI, then getting involved in open-source projects could be your next big move.

Getting Started with Open Source

The first step is understanding what open source entails. It's about more than just accessing free software or tools. It's about contributing to the development of cutting-edge technologies. Imagine you're using a piece of AI software and notice a bug or think of a feature to enhance it. In the open-source world, you can do something about it. You can modify the code, add features, or improve functionality and share your improvements with the community. To get started, platforms like GitHub, GitLab, and Bitbucket are your gateways. They host thousands of projects ranging from fledgling programs developed by hobbyists to significant tools used by large corporations. Many of these projects welcome contributions from anyone willing to help, regardless of their level of expertise.

Benefits of Contribution

Contributing to open-source AI projects offers a multitude of benefits. For starters, it's a powerful way to develop your skills. As you dive into the code and solve real-world problems, you'll learn new programming languages, tools, and technologies at a pace that classroom learning can't match. Then there's the networking aspect. Collaborating on projects connects you with other AI enthusiasts and professionals from around the globe. These connections can lead to job opportunities, collaborations, or valuable friendships. Moreover, your contributions to open-source projects are a publicly visible portfolio of your skills and dedication to AI, which can significantly boost your professional profile.

Finding Projects and Making Contributions

Finding the right project can feel like looking for a needle in a haystack, given the sheer number of open-source initiatives. Start by aligning your search with your interests in AI–be it neural networks, natural language processing, or robotics. Websites like GitHub Explore can help you filter projects by language, technology, and popularity. Once you find a project that resonates with you, start small. Begin by understanding the project's contribution guidelines, typically found in a file named CONTRIBUTING.md in the project repository. Then, look at the 'Issues' section of the repository to find tasks suitable for newcomers. These tasks often have tags like 'good first issue' or 'help wanted.' Tackling these minor issues allows you to get familiar with the project without overwhelming you.

Whether you're looking to sharpen your programming skills, build your professional network, or contribute to meaningful technology, the open-source community welcomes all willing to learn and help. So why not dive in? Your next contribution could be the start of something big.

9.3 STAYING UPDATED: FOLLOWING AI TRENDS AND INNOVATIONS

In the fast-paced world of artificial intelligence, staying updated isn't just a nice-to-have; it's essential for anyone looking to remain relevant and innovative. Think of AI as a river that's constantly flowing and changing course. If you need to keep an eye on the current, you might find yourself swimming upstream. Several resources are explicitly designed to keep you informed and ahead of the curve in AI.

You're spoilt for choice when it comes to reliable sources for AI news and updates, but discernment is key. Websites like 'MIT Technology Review' offer deep dives into the latest tech advancements and ethical discussions surrounding AI, and for those who prefer a more scientific approach, journals like 'The Journal of Artificial Intelligence Research' provide peer-reviewed articles that can give you a more technical understanding of ongoing research. There are also influencers and thought leaders on platforms like Twitter and LinkedIn—following folks like Andrew Ng or Fei-Fei Li can provide insightful commentary and foresight into where AI is headed next. For more interactive content, podcasts such as 'AI in Business' blend expert interviews with practical applications of AI in various industries, making complex topics digestible and engaging.

But staying updated isn't just about passively consuming information but actively engaging with new knowledge. This is where continuous learning comes into play.

Online Learning Platforms

The field of AI offers an abundance of online courses ranging from beginner to advanced levels. Platforms like Coursera and Udacity offer courses in partnership with leading universities and companies, ensuring you're learning the latest and most relevant content. The landscape of education is continually evolving, with online learning platforms playing a pivotal role in this transformation. These platforms provide accessible, flexible, and diverse educational opportunities, catering to learners from all walks of life. Among the myriad of options available, platforms like Coursera, Udemy, and W3Schools stand out due to their unique offerings and approaches to online education.

Coursera: Founded by two Stanford professors, Coursera partners with universities and organizations worldwide to offer a wide range of courses, specializations, and degrees across a multitude of subjects. This platform is particularly known for its strong academic foundations and collaborations with prestigious institutions, which enable learners to access high-quality educational content and earn recognized credentials.

Udemy: Udemy serves as a massive marketplace for learning and teaching online, where individuals can create courses on topics they are passionate about and learners can enhance their skills at their own pace. With a focus on professional and personal development, Udemy offers courses in a variety of areas, including technology, business, arts, and more. This platform is distinguished by its vast selection and the opportunity for experts in any field to share their knowledge.

W3Schools: As a leading web developer information website, W3Schools offers free tutorials and references on web development languages such as HTML, CSS, JavaScript, PHP, SQL, and much more. This platform is especially favored by beginners in the web development field due to its straightforward, easy-to-understand instructional style and practical approach to learning. W3Schools is an invaluable resource for anyone looking to start or enhance their skills in web development.

One of the best aspects of these online programs is their ability to be updated with the latest rapidly changing information. Also, in addition to the courses you'll find, there are webinars and workshops that can address the latest topics and allow for real-time interaction with experts. These sessions provide fresh knowledge, clarify doubts, and offer new perspectives, keeping your learning dynamic and current.

Applying the latest knowledge from these trends and updates to your projects or work can be incredibly rewarding. Say you come across a new algorithm that speeds up data processing. Implementing this in your next project could enhance efficiency and give you a tangible edge over competitors. During a webinar, you can also learn about a new AI application in customer service. Testing this out could significantly enhance user satisfaction and streamline operations. Always look for practical applications of the knowledge you gain. This could involve experimenting with new tools or techniques or integrating fresh insights into your strategic planning.

Forecasting future trends in AI is another critical aspect of staying updated. You can predict where AI is headed by analyzing current trends and technological advancements. For example, the increasing focus on ethical AI suggests that future developments prioritize transparency and fairness in AI algorithms. Similarly, integrating AI with emerging technologies like IoT and blockchain hints at a future where AI will be even more interconnected with our daily lives. Understanding these trajectories can help you prepare for future shifts in the tech landscape, ensuring that you or your business is always a step ahead.

Keeping your finger on the pulse of AI innovations and trends is about strategically gathering, learning, and applying knowledge. It's about being proactive in your educational pursuits and creatively using your insights, ensuring you remain a valuable player in AI. Whether you're a developer, a business owner, or simply an AI enthusiast, staying updated is your bridge to not just keeping up with AI developments but actively participating in shaping them.

9.4 ATTENDING AI WORKSHOPS AND CONFERENCES FOR BEGINNERS

Diving into the world of AI can be as thrilling as it is daunting, especially if you're at the beginning of your AI learning path. Workshops and conferences offer a fantastic opportunity to immerse yourself in the field. Still, the key is choosing the right ones that align with your current knowledge level and learning goals. For beginners, it's essential to select events that provide introductory content and foundational knowledge rather than those tailored for advanced practitioners, which might delve into complexities that could be overwhelming at this stage. So, how do you pick the right events? Start by identifying what you hope to gain—understanding AI basics, learning about specific AI applications in your field, or networking with AI professionals. Then, research events that match these criteria and check their agendas to ensure they include beginner-friendly sessions.

Once you've chosen an event, the next step is to make the most out of it. Before the event:

1. Prepare by familiarizing yourself with basic AI concepts and/or the speakers' backgrounds. This preparation will allow you to engage more effectively during sessions and understand the context of discussions.

2. Feel free to ask questions or participate in discussions during the event.

3. Remember, the goal is to learn, and clarifying your doubts is crucial to the learning process.

4. Make a point to interact with other attendees.

Networking is not just about exchanging business cards; it's about sharing ideas and experiences. Who knows? The person you speak with might have the insights you need to move forward in your AI journey or could be a future collaborator.

Considering the current global scenario, many events offer virtual and in-person formats. Each has its pros and cons. Virtual events are accessible from anywhere in the world, providing flexibility and saving you the time and expense of travel. They often feature recordings of sessions that you can revisit at your convenience. However, they need more personal touch and networking opportunities offered by in-person events. In contrast, attending an event in person allows for spontaneous interactions and can be more engaging. The choice between virtual and in-person should depend on what you value more—convenience, access to information, or the depth of personal interaction.

Lastly, for those just starting their AI adventure, here are a few notable AI workshops and conferences that are known to be beginner-friendly:

- **AI for All**: This conference is designed for those new to AI. It covers basic concepts and applications of AI in various industries. The sessions are structured to help beginners grasp the fundamentals of AI without getting lost in technical jargon.

- **TechTalks AI Conference**: Known for its wide range of topics, this conference offers specific tracks for beginners. It's a great place to start if you're exploring different areas of AI or finding which niche might interest you the most.

- **Global AI Bootcamp** is a worldwide event that brings together AI enthusiasts to learn about AI from the basics through hands-on workshops and sessions. It's beneficial for practical learning and application.

Each of these events is structured to help you learn about AI and experience it through practical, interactive sessions that cater to beginners. By carefully selecting suitable events and actively engaging in them, you can significantly enhance your understanding of AI and lay a solid foundation for your future in this exciting field.

9.5 NETWORKING TIPS FOR AI ENTHUSIASTS

Navigating the networking landscape as an AI enthusiast can feel like jumping into a dynamic, ever-evolving ecosystem. It's a place where forging the right connections can enhance your learning curve and propel your career forward in unexpected and exciting ways. Let's break down some effective strategies for maximizing your networking efforts within the AI community.

First, approaching experts and peers in the field might seem daunting, but remember, the AI community is generally collaborative and open to sharing knowledge. A good starting point is to engage with the content shared online–whether it's a groundbreaking research paper, a thought-provoking blog post, or even a tweet about the latest AI trends. Commenting with insightful observations or thoughtful questions can initiate a dialogue and gradually build rapport. When attending conferences or workshops, don't hesitate to ask speakers questions during Q&A sessions or follow up with them afterward to express your interest in their work and discuss common professional interests. Taking a proactive approach can transform a fleeting interaction into a meaningful connection.

Building meaningful connections in the AI field hinges on mutual learning and collaboration. It's not just about exchanging business cards; it's about exchanging ideas, challenges, and experiences. When you meet someone new, focus on how you can help them as much as how they can help you. Perhaps you've encountered a solution to a problem they're currently facing, or you've come across a resource that could benefit their work. Sharing these without expecting anything can cultivate goodwill and lay the foundation for a solid professional relationship. Additionally, consider collaborating on projects or co-authoring articles. These joint ventures can deepen your connection and allow you to learn from each other's expertise.

In today's digital age, online networking opportunities are abundant. Platforms like LinkedIn, Twitter, and specialized forums on sites like Stack Overflow or GitHub are bustling with AI professionals and enthusiasts from around the globe. Joining LinkedIn groups or Twitter chats focused on AI can give you access to a diverse network of individuals who share your passion for artificial intelligence. Participating in these online communities by sharing your insights, asking questions, and contributing to discussions can raise your profile within the community. Virtual meetups and webinars also offer opportunities to connect with like-minded professionals in a more structured setting. These platforms often feature breakout sessions or discussion groups for more personal interaction.

Leveraging your network effectively can lead to substantial career growth. Your connections can open doors to job opportunities, collaborative projects, and mentorship. If you're looking for a mentor, for instance, identify professionals who have the expertise and the inclination to guide others. When reaching out, specify why you're seeking their mentorship and what you hope to learn from them. For job opportunities, keep your LinkedIn profile updated with your latest projects and skills, and inform your connections when you're looking for new challenges. Often, jobs in the tech field are filled through referrals, so having a robust network can significantly enhance your job prospects.

Navigating the networking maze in the AI community with these strategies can transform your professional journey, opening and expanding new avenues for learning and growth. Engaging actively, building mutually beneficial relationships, and leveraging online platforms are key steps in cultivating a network that supports your current professional needs and paves the way for future opportunities.

Networking is not just a peripheral component of your professional life; it's a powerful catalyst for growth, innovation, and opportunity.

CHAPTER 10:
LOOKING AHEAD: THE FUTURE AND ETHICS OF AI

I've touched on the Ethics of AI throughout this book, but let's look a little deeper.

We're on the brink of some genuinely titanic technological shifts. If you're as curious about these innovations as I am, you're in for a real treat. Let's dive into what's next for AI, exploring the cool, shiny gadgets and the profound impacts these technologies are poised to have on our world.

10.1 PREDICTING THE NEXT BIG THING IN AI

Innovative Technologies on the Horizon

So, what's the next big wave in AI that we should all be watching? Every day, there seems to be a new breakthrough, but some of the most thrilling developments push the boundaries of what we believe AI can do. Take, for example, the rise of emotionally intelligent AI that can understand and process human emotions. This isn't just about recognizing a smile or a frown; it's about AI that can interpret the subtleties of human expressions and respond in emotionally intelligent ways. This leap could revolutionize everything from customer service bots that genuinely empathize with your frustrations to mental health apps that provide support by reading emotional cues that even humans might miss.

Another frontier is AI in creative industries. We're not just talking about AI that can play chess or write a decent pop song. The horizon is lit with AI that collaborates with artists and designers to push creative boundaries, blending human imagination with AI's immense processing power to create art, music, and literature that might be impossible for working solo.

Impact of Quantum Computing

Quantum computing is set to turbocharge AI's capabilities. If you think quantum physics sounds like something out of a sci-fi novel, you're not alone. But here's the scoop: quantum computers can process complex data at speeds unimaginable with current technology. For AI, this means faster learning and improved efficiency. These advancements could tackle some of our toughest challenges, from environmental preservation to disease treatment, at speeds that today's computers can only dream of.

AI and Augmented Reality

Augmented reality (AR) and AI are becoming an increasingly dynamic duo, especially in fields like education, healthcare, and entertainment. AR overlays digital information in the real world. When powered by AI, this technology can adapt to the environment and the user's needs in real time. Consider an AR application that not only shows a mechanic how to fix an engine but adapts the tutorial to the specific problem, the mechanic's skill level, and even their learning style, all processed in real time by AI. Or think about medical students using AR to practice surgeries, with AI providing real-time feedback, simulating different scenarios, and enhancing the learning experience. The possibilities for AR and AI to transform how we learn, work, and play are limitless.

As we look ahead to the unfolding landscape of AI, it's clear that the innovations on the horizon are as exciting as they are impactful. From transforming creative industries to making strides in sustainability, the subsequent developments in AI are set to redefine the boundaries of technology and its role in our lives. So, whether you're a businessperson looking to leverage AI for competitive advantage, a creative soul excited about the new tools at your disposal, or simply someone curious about the future of tech, the coming changes promise something for everyone. Stay tuned and stay curious. Everyone will feel the impact, and if we pay attention to current trends, we have a chance to understand what's coming and how to best adapt to it.

10.2 Ethical Use of AI: Guidelines and Best Practices

Navigating the complex world of AI ethics can sometimes feel like walking through a maze—there are many paths, not all of them clear, and the stakes are high. But don't worry; you're not alone in this. Across the globe, tech leaders, ethicists, and policymakers are crafting frameworks and guidelines to ensure AI develops in ways that benefit society while minimizing harm. These frameworks aren't just about avoiding bad press; they're about fostering trust and ensuring the sustainable growth of AI technologies for the betterment of humanity. Let's unpack some of these guidelines and see how they can be applied in everyday AI scenarios.

Developing ethical AI starts with a robust framework. Think of this as a blueprint that guides every stage of AI development, from initial design to deployment and beyond. One well-regarded example is the Ethics Guidelines for Trustworthy AI developed by the European Commission. This framework outlines seven essential requirements that AI systems should meet to be deemed trustworthy: transparency, fairness, and accountability. Adopting such a framework doesn't just help mitigate risks; it also aligns AI practices with broader societal values and legal norms, making AI products more acceptable to users and regulators.

Moving on, transparency in AI is crucial. It's about shedding light on how AI systems make decisions. Why is this important? We want to avoid bias as much as possible, and when users understand how an AI system works, they can trust it more. But transparency isn't just about user trust; it's also about accountability. When an AI system makes a decision, especially with significant implications, like in healthcare diagnosis or legal settings, it's vital to trace how that decision was made. For instance, if an AI system denies someone a loan or a critical medical procedure, the operators should be able to identify why this decision was made and ensure it wasn't due to a system error or bias.

Despite the best efforts of developers, AI systems can still inherit or even amplify human biases present in their training data or algorithms. This can lead to unfair treatment of certain groups, undermining both the utility and fairness of AI applications. Addressing this challenge involves rigorous testing and continuous monitoring to ensure AI systems operate as intended. For example, before deploying an AI recruitment tool, testing it across diverse demographic groups is critical to ensure it doesn't favor one group over another unfairly. Moreover, deploying fairness-enhancing techniques, such as adjusting the data used for training the AI or tweaking the algorithm itself, can correct biases detected during these tests or, if done unethically, make them worse.

Lastly, let's touch on privacy and data protection. With AI systems processing vast amounts of personal data to learn and make decisions, safeguarding this data is paramount. For instance, the General Data Protection Regulation (GDPR) in Europe provides a robust data protection framework. It sets the standard for collecting, using, and storing personal data and empowers individuals by granting them rights over their data. AI developers can adhere to these principles by implementing data minimization strategies, ensuring data is collected and stored only when necessary, and protecting it from unauthorized access through state-of-the-art security measures.

Navigating the ethical landscape of AI requires a commitment to these principles throughout the lifecycle of AI systems. By embedding ethical considerations into the DNA of AI development processes, businesses can create AI solutions that are not only innovative and efficient but also responsible and trustworthy. This commitment to ethics is not just about doing good; it's also about doing well in a world that increasingly values ethical considerations in technology.

10.3 THE DO'S AND DON'TS OF GENERATIVE AI

Navigating the realm of generative AI is akin to exploring a vibrant city filled with endless possibilities but also with its own set of rules and guidelines. As you delve into creating and utilizing generative AI, it's crucial to tread thoughtfully, ensuring that your innovative endeavors are productive and responsible. Let's talk about what this looks like, starting with creating and using AI technologies. Imagine you're crafting a piece of generative AI that can write poetry. The first rule of thumb is to respect intellectual property. Your AI should generate original content and not just rehash lines from well-known poets without proper credit. This respect extends to the datasets you train your AI on—ensuring that the data used is rightfully yours, publicly available, or used under license.

Misinformation is another critical area of concern. In an age where information spreads in seconds, the potential for AI-generated content to mislead or deceive, even unintentionally, is high. To mitigate this, you should implement checks to ensure the accuracy of the content your AI produces. For example, if your AI writes news articles, setting up a review system with fact-checking outputs can help maintain credibility and trust. Moreover, the implications of the content being generated should be considered. If the AI is creating medical advice, the accuracy of information becomes not just a matter of ethics but of public safety. Ensuring that qualified professionals oversee such content is paramount.

Moving on to avoiding misuse, the power of generative AI to create realistic content can be a double-edged sword. Take deepfakes, for instance. These videos or audio recordings look and sound like real people saying or doing things they never did. While the technology behind deepfakes can be used for legitimate purposes like entertainment (think of rejuvenating actors in movies or creating realistic avatars for video games), the potential for harm is significant. To combat this, developing and using generative AI responsibly involves clear labeling of AI-generated content. This transparency lets users understand that what they see or hear may not be genuine, thus preventing deception. Furthermore, developers should consider building safeguards that can detect and deter the malicious use of their technologies, such as watermarking content or embedding other forms of detectable metadata.

Adhering to legal and ethical standards cannot be overstated. As generative AI's capabilities expand, so does the need for robust legal frameworks to govern its use. Staying informed about the laws and regulations that apply to AI in your country or industry is crucial. This includes copyright laws, data protection regulations, and any specific AI and digital content legislation. Beyond legal compliance, adhering to ethical standards involves considering the broader impacts of your AI systems. For instance, if your generative AI is used in recruitment, ensuring it does not perpetuate biases or discriminate against certain groups is crucial. This ethical commitment might involve regular audits of your AI systems to check for biases and take corrective actions if necessary.

As you continue to explore and innovate within the bounds of generative AI, keeping these do's and don'ts in mind ensures that your journey is not only creatively rewarding but also ethically sound and legally compliant.

10.4 HOW TO STAY AHEAD IN THE FAST-EVOLVING AI LANDSCAPE

Staying ahead in the fast-paced world of AI is like trying to surf on the crest of a wave; it's thrilling, a bit risky, and requires constant motion and adaptation. If you're aiming to ride this wave and steer it, embracing the ethos of continuous learning is non-negotiable. AI isn't a field where you can learn a few skills and then rest on your laurels. AI technology evolves too quickly for that. What's cutting-edge today might be old news tomorrow. Think of continuous learning as your ongoing ticket to the AI show. It involves regularly updating your knowledge base and skills through various channels, whether taking online courses, attending workshops, or simply setting aside time each week to read up on the latest research and trends.

This approach doesn't just keep you relevant; it deepens your understanding and enhances your ability to innovate. For instance, if you're a business professional using AI for data analysis, staying updated on the latest algorithms could dramatically increase the accuracy of your insights, giving your business a competitive edge. Or, if you're in a creative field, new AI tools could create new ways of generating designs or music, keeping your work fresh and exciting. The key here is to establish a routine or system that integrates learning into your daily or weekly schedule. As mentioned earlier, platforms like Coursera and Udacity and AI-focused publications like 'Synced' or 'The Algorithm newsletter' by MIT Technology Review can be invaluable resources in this journey.

While digging into books and tutorials is great, remember the power of collaboration and networking. The AI community is remarkably dynamic, and the exchange of ideas within this community can spark new ways of thinking and unexpected opportunities. Engaging with other AI professionals allows you to share your challenges and successes, get feedback on your work, and gain insights you might have yet to consider.

Amid all this learning and networking, another crucial element is innovative thinking. This means not just applying AI technologies but thinking about how they can be used in new, groundbreaking ways. It's about looking at problems from a fresh perspective and daring to experiment with solutions that others might not have considered. Say you're working with AI in retail; innovative thinking might lead you to explore how AI can enhance in-store experiences rather than just online interactions, perhaps through personalized shopping assistants or smart mirrors that offer fashion advice. Beyond using AI for patient diagnosis, you might explore its preventive potential by predicting disease outbreaks or personalizing patient health plans based on extensive data analysis.

Encouraging a culture of experimentation within your team or company can also lead to significant innovations. This could be as simple as dedicating time each week to brainstorming sessions where every idea is too outlandish to consider or setting up 'hackathons' where your team works intensively to develop new AI-driven solutions to business problems. This kind of environment fosters creative thinking and can lead to developments that give your company an edge in the competitive AI landscape.

Whether developing new AI technologies or leveraging existing ones in your business or creative endeavors, these principles will ensure you remain at the forefront of the AI revolution, riding the wave of technological advancement with confidence and creativity.

10.5 THE ROLE OF AI IN SHAPING FUTURE SOCIETIES

As we peer into the future, it's clear that AI is not just a tool in our technological arsenal—it's a transformative force poised to profoundly reshape our societies. The economic landscape, for instance, is on the brink of significant transformation powered by AI. Picture this: a future where AI doesn't just automate tasks but creates entirely new categories of jobs and, in the process, redefines existing ones. It's an exciting, albeit daunting, prospect. AI-driven technologies like machine learning and robotics are already streamlining manufacturing, logistics, and customer service operations. But the impact goes beyond just making businesses more efficient.

Consider the rise of new job categories such as AI trainers, who teach AI systems how to recognize and process information correctly, or AI ethicists, who help companies navigate the complex moral landscapes that AI ventures into. These roles were virtually nonexistent a decade ago. On the flip side, there's a genuine concern about job displacement. As AI becomes capable of performing complex tasks, traditionally human-held roles are being automated. However, this shift can also be seen as an opportunity for workforce transformation, where the focus shifts from manual, repetitive tasks to more strategic and creative roles. The key to managing this transition effectively lies in education and training programs that can equip workers with the skills needed to thrive in an AI-driven economy.

The future of human-AI interaction presents a tapestry of opportunities woven with challenges. As AI systems become more autonomous and integrated into daily life, how we interact with these technologies—and how they interact with us—will evolve. Imagine AI personal assistants that manage your schedule and provide companionship or AI-driven platforms that personalize your educational experience, adapting content to match your learning pace and style. These interactions promise to make our lives more convenient and personalized. Still, they also raise important questions about privacy, security, and the changing nature of human relationships.

How we navigate these challenges will significantly shape the societal impact of AI. It is crucial to ensure that AI systems are designed with human-centric principles at heart. This means developing AI technologies that enhance human capabilities and foster positive relationships rather than creating dependency or isolation. As AI becomes a more prominent fixture in our lives, maintaining a dialogue between technology developers, policymakers, and the public will be key to achieving a balanced integration of AI that respects and enhances human dignity and autonomy.

From economic transformations to ethical governance and human interaction, AI holds the potential to redefine the fabric of our societies. How we harness this potential will determine the legacy of AI in our collective future.

CONCLUSION:

Wow, what a journey we've been on together! From the get-go, we dove into the fascinating world of Generative AI, unpacking its complex concepts and making them understandable and engaging. We explored its transformative impact across various fields—writing, art, music, voice generation, and even robust business strategies. Whether you were crafting a haunting melody with AIVA or shaping engaging marketing content with Jasper, the journey through each chapter wasn't just about learning—it was about experiencing the power of AI firsthand.

Reflecting on our adventure, one of the key takeaways has been the incredible democratization of AI technology. No matter your background—be it a seasoned tech enthusiast or a curious newcomer—the tools and insights shared here were designed to make AI not only accessible but also a potent part of your creative and professional arsenal. The goal was to peel back the intimidating layers of AI and show you that with the proper guidance, these tools are as accessible as they are powerful.

But here's the thing—the world of AI doesn't stand still, and neither should you. I encourage you to keep the flame of curiosity alive; continue exploring, experimenting, and pushing the boundaries of what you can create and innovate with AI. The landscape of artificial intelligence is rapidly evolving, and staying informed is your best tool for harnessing its potential to the fullest.

Beyond the practical applications, there's an equally important narrative that needs your voice—the discussion on the ethical use of AI. This discussion needs your engagement with the community, your contributions to conversations, and your efforts to steer the future of AI. Being involved and not just sitting on the sidelines helps with the future for everyone.

Imagine a future where AI further revolutionizes how we express ourselves creatively, optimize business operations, and even manage personal lives. It's a future ripe with possibilities, limited only by our imagination and willingness to continue learning and adapting.

As we wrap up this book, I hope it is a valuable steppingstone in your AI journey. May it inspire you to explore beyond the horizon and leverage AI in ways we have yet to envision. Dive into this ongoing adventure with enthusiasm and confidence, knowing you're equipped to make the most of what AI offers.

I'd love to hear how this book has impacted your journey into AI, and I'd really appreciate your positive review on Amazon or wherever you bought it. Your feedback, stories, or questions are not just welcome; they're eagerly anticipated.

Here's to you and your future in the exhilarating world of AI—may it be as limitless as your potential to innovate and transform. Your journey is not just about exploring and creating; it's about dreaming big and making those dreams a reality with the power of AI. Keep exploring, keep creating, and most importantly, keep dreaming big.

Make a Difference with Your Review

Now that you've learned how to harness the power of Generative AI, it's time to spread the word and keep the momentum going.

Please Leave a Review to Help Others...

By sharing your thoughts about this book on Amazon, **you help other AI enthusiasts discover this valuable resource.** Your opinion could be the signpost for someone else's journey into Generative AI.

Thank you for your assistance and for reading my book; I truly hope it was the Playbook you needed right now. The spirit of **Generative AI thrives on shared knowledge**, and your review helps ensure that more people benefit from this technology.

****Type in the URL or Scan the QR code to Leave a Review

https://amzn.to/4bVeDwT

By helping to pass on what you've learned, **you're playing a crucial role in keeping the Generative AI community vibrant and growing.**

Thank you for being part of this journey.

All the best to you in your AI future,

Branson Adams

REFERENCES

1. Microsoft Cloud Advocates (n.d.). *Generative AI for Beginners (Version 2) - A Course* [MOOC]. Retrieved from https://microsoft.github.io/generative-ai-for-beginners/

2. Wikipedia contributors. (n.d.). Generative adversarial network. In *Wikipedia, The Free Encyclopedia*. https://en.wikipedia.org/wiki/Generative_adversarial_network

3. Coursera. (2024). *Deep Learning vs. Machine Learning: A Beginner's Guide*. Retrieved from https://www.coursera.org/articles/ai-vs-deep-learning-vs-machine-learning-beginners-guide

4. Marr, B. (2023, November 30). *Generative AI And The Future Of Content Creation*. Forbes. Retrieved from https://www.forbes.com/sites/bernardmarr/2023/11/30/generative-ai-and-the-future-of-content-creation/

5. One Art Nation. (2024.). *How AI Is Transforming the Art Market*. Retrieved from https://www.oneartnation.com/how-ai-is-transforming-the-art-market/

6. Andreessen Horowitz. (2023). *The Future of Music: How Generative AI Is Transforming the Music Industry*. Retrieved from https://a16z.com/the-future-of-music-how-generative-ai-is-transforming-the-music-industry/

7. Speechify. (n.d.). *Exploring AI Animation: A Generative Leap Forward*. Retrieved from https://speechify.com/blog/ai-animation/

8. Zapier. (n.d.). *How to use Jasper AI as your writing assistant*. Retrieved from https://zapier.com/blog/jasper-ai/

9. GitHub. (n.d.). *Getting started with GitHub Copilot*. Retrieved from https://docs.github.com/en/copilot/using-github-copilot/getting-started-with-github-copilot

10. Involve.me. (n.d.). *5 Ways to Use AI Tools to Boost Your Brand Storytelling*. Retrieved from https://www.involve.me/blog/5-ways-to-use-ai-tools-to-boost-your-brand-storytelling

11. University of Michigan-Dearborn. (n.d.). *Generative AI Prompt Engineering*. Retrieved from https://umdearborn.edu/digital-education/generative-ai-um-dearborn/generative-ai-prompt-engineering

12. Looka. (n.d.). *Logo Design & Brand Identity for Entrepreneurs*. Retrieved from https://looka.com

13. Incredimate. (n.d.). *What You Need to Know About AI Animation: Techniques, Tools, and Trends*. Retrieved from https://www.incredimate.com/blog/ai-animation-techniques-tools-and-trends

14. Creative AIs. (2023). *AIVA AI Music Generator: Getting Started*. Retrieved from https://creativeais.com/aiva-ai-music-generator/

15. Deepgram. (2023). *State of Voice Technology 2023*. Retrieved from https://deepgram.com/state-of-voice-technology-2023

16. RSS. (2024). *The Best AI Tools for Podcasting - And How To Use Them*. Retrieved from https://rss.com/blog/the-best-ai-tools-for-podcasting-and-how-to-use-them/

17. Reedsy Blog. (n.d.). *How to Record an Audiobook with AI in 6 Steps*. Retrieved from https://blog.reedsy.com/guide/audiobooks/ai-narration/

18. Sound Tech Insider. (2023). *AIVA Review - Everything You Need To Know - AI Composition*. Retrieved from

https://soundtechinsider.com/aiva-review-everything-you-need-to-know-ai-composition

19. Mosaic. (n.d.). *A Guide to Using AI for Financial Modeling & Forecasting*. Retrieved from https://www.mosaic.tech/ai-in-finance/modeling-forecasting

20. Sendbird. (2024.). The ultimate guide to AI customer service chatbots. Retrieved from https://sendbird.com/blog/ultimate-guide-to-ai-customer-service-chatbots

21. PixelPlex. (2023). *7 Predictive Analytics Examples: From Marketing to Finance and Healthcare,* Retrieved from https://pixelplex.io/blog/predictive-analytics-examples/

22. Mailmodo. (n.d.). *10 Real-Life AI Marketing Examples and Use Cases*. Retrieved from https://www.mailmodo.com/guides/ai-in-marketing-examples/

23. Well+Good. (n.d.). *AI Is Making Personalized Fitness Even Smarter*. Retrieved from https://www.wellandgood.com/ai-personalized-fitness

24. Ling App. (2024). *6 Best AI Language Learning Apps In 2024!* Retrieved from https://ling-app.com/tips/best-ai-language-learning-apps/

25. GeeksforGeeks. (2024). *10 Top AI Tools for Personal Finance Management and Budgeting - 2024*. Retrieved from https://www.geeksforgeeks.org/ai-tools-for-personal-finance-management-and-budgeting/

Made in the USA
Las Vegas, NV
17 October 2024

97008733R00079